SOUL
STRENGTH

DISCOVERY
JOURNAL

SOUL
STRENGTH

DISCOVERY
JOURNAL

DR. ALAN AHLGRIM

ILLUMIFY
MEDIA.COM

SOUL
STRENGTH

DISCOVERY
JOURNAL

Published by
Illumify Media Global
www.IllumifyMedia.com
"Let's bring your book to life!"

Paperback ISBN: 978-1-955043-11-3

Typeset by Art Innovations (http://artinnovations.in/)
Cover design by Debbie Lewis

Printed in the United States of America

CONTENTS

INTRODUCTION

I love new beginnings!

There's something especially exciting about making a fresh start and launching a new adventure. The *Discovery Journal* you hold in your hands is just that. This is an enriching resource to help make soul care sustainable even for those who don't see themselves as the journaling type, or even the praying type.

I'm out to demystify journaling and prayer. You don't have to live in a monastery or have two uninterrupted hours every morning to find soul-enriching benefits. Just begin here and begin with this resource.

If possible, don't begin it alone.

It's been said that the difference between a trip and a pilgrimage is that a pilgrimage changes you. Soul care is a pilgrimage. And every journey is made richer by the people who travel with you.

Imagine taking an extended tour of an intriguing location but taking it alone. Now, imagine taking that as a pilgrimage with others who might be changed by it as well. Every insight, delight and discovery would be amplified. Each of your companions would at times spot things you had missed, and all your friends would appreciate sharing their highlights with one another in unhurried conversations along the way—and long after as well.

A soul-enriching pilgrimage isn't a solo affair. We all need others to grow along with us.

We also need a guide to help us get the best out of the experience. Consider this *Discovery Journal* to be your guide. It is intended to be your soul care companion for the immediate future.

Using this journal isn't intended to be a rigid experience. You can use it daily on your own for twelve weeks, or any period that works best for you. It was, however, designed to provide a relational experience, so I encourage you to invite friends or members of a small group to embark on this adventure with you.

I wish someone had provided something like this for me decades ago. I long struggled with disappointment over my prayer and devotional life. What I needed was a simple guidebook to use with my Bible. I needed someone to help me see that prayer isn't just a verbal monologue but a free-flowing conversational experience throughout the day. I needed to see that journaling wasn't just about extensive navel gazing when I was discouraged and confused, but rather an opportunity to daily jot a few sentences to clarify my thoughts and praises.

So, here's that resource. Consider it a soul care track for you to run on. And here are a few suggestions to enhance the journey:

1. The *Discovery Journal* is designed to be used in conjunction with a companion book, *Soul Strength: Rhythms for Thriving*, which contains 12 transcendent soul care principles that will challenge and encourage you. Read a chapter a week, or go at your own pace.

2. Set aside ten to fifteen minutes a day for quiet reading and reflection. Use the journal questions to help you as you seek to discover your daily AHA!

3. Invite one to four others to join you. Keep your soul care circle tight.

4. Schedule a weekly or monthly gathering for an enriching in-depth conversation. Choose a private location, not simply a crowded coffee shop or restaurant. People don't go deep in the middle of Denny's!

5. For those seeking even greater transformational benefit, pursue the possibility of joining a three-year journey with a covenant group. Information on these small gatherings of Christian leaders is available through Covenant Connections ministry. All groups follow the same simple template: Four members, over three years, with two retreats per year and one video connection per month. Four, three, two, one!

Who cares about your soul care? While the care of your soul is first and foremost your responsibility, you still need others in your life to sharpen, enlighten and encourage you. When you dare to open your soul to others, a whole new world will open for you!

By the way, each time I meet with a small group, we begin our session by checking in with a word or phrase that describes how we're feeling. We follow that with a personal declaration: "I'm all in!"

Here's a sample of the sorts of things I and others have said:

- *I'm hopeful … and I'm all in!*
- *I'm exhausted … but I'm all in!*
- *I'm distracted … but I'm trying to be all in!*
- *I'm thriving … and I'm all in!*

The declaration says to yourself and to others, *Life isn't perfect, I'm not perfect, but I'm present and engaged.*

After the declaration, others in the group respond, "Blessings be on you!"

Now it's your turn! Respond with how you're feeling today, along with your willingness to be present and engaged:

I'm _____ and/but I'm all in!

May God's richest blessings be on you!

Now let's get started.

1

EMBRACE YOUR STORY

Read Chapter 1 from the book, Soul Strength: Rhythms for Thriving.

One of my business buddies shared with me how a breakthrough happened with a new team he was managing at work. He decided to take a relational approach and have everyone take turns sharing their life stories over a series of no-agenda dinners in a relaxed setting.

The results amazed him. One person said, "I've never had a manager who cared to know about the challenges I faced as an insecure teenager moving here from another country. Thank you."

As acquaintances and colleagues shared personal stories, individuals felt deeply heard and valued—and that wasn't where the benefit ended. The entire team bonded more deeply as well.

This wasn't a strange phenomenon. Our stories connect us. I'm sure you've had an experience or two that confirms this truth.

Sharing our stories doesn't always come naturally. Sometimes we are tempted to stay silent and even invisible. But if we give in to that temptation, everyone loses.

ENJOY THE FOLLOWING REFLECTIONS:

- ☐ Reflect on Our Stories
- ☐ Reflect on Vulnerability
- ☐ Reflect on Truthfulness
- ☐ Reflect on Going Small
- ☐ Reflect on Value
- ☐ Sabbath Reflection

"

GOD IS OUR MERCIFUL
FATHER AND THE SOURCE
OF ALL COMFORT. HE
COMFORTS US IN ALL OUR
TROUBLES SO THAT WE CAN
COMFORT OTHERS.

(2 CORINTHIANS 1:3-4)

"

REFLECT ON OUR STORIES

At a weekend retreat, seven men became a band of brothers.

The more everyone shared in depth, the more everyone felt connected.

After sharing a heartbreaking story, one man named Doug added, "I'm fifty-four, and I've never felt that I belonged until now."

The truth is that we don't want another entertaining talk. Everyone is weary of words. We are all inundated with information. Great books, blogs, and podcasts abound. We're gluttons when it comes to content, but we're starving for heartfelt truth and in-depth conversation.

We're in desperate need of knowing that we're not alone in the journey of life. When you have personally struggled with tough stuff, don't be afraid to own it and share it with others. The stories we tell that we truly own—because they *are* our own—will always have the greatest impact on others.

READ THE VERSE ON THE OPPOSITE PAGE, THEN REPHRASE AND PERSONALIZE AS A PRAYER FROM YOU TO GOD.

Q: A:

On a scale of 1 to 10, how open
are you to sharing stories of your
personal struggles with others?
What kinds of struggles are you
willing to talk about? Are there
struggles you want to keep secret?

Q: A:

What memory do you have of
being vulnerable with someone
who responded well to what
you shared? What memory do
you have of a time someone
responded hurtfully? Has either of
those experiences impacted how
willing you are to share now?

Q: A:

If you have stories you have never
shared with anyone, as you ponder
those stories, what thoughts or
emotions do you experience?

MY "AHA"

WAKEN

WHAT PASSAGE OR INSIGHT FELT MOST PERSONAL FOR YOU?

HEAR

WHAT MIGHT GOD BE SAYING TO YOU?

ASK

WRITE A PRAYER ASKING GOD TO HELP YOU EMBRACE THE VALUE OF YOUR STORY TO BRING BLESSING INTO YOUR LIFE OR INTO THE LIFE OF SOMEONE YOU KNOW.

"

EVERYTHING THAT HAS
HAPPENED TO ME HERE HAS
HELPED TO SPREAD THE
GOOD NEWS.

(PHILIPPIANS 1:12)

"

*The apostle Paul wrote this
while suffering in prison.*

REFLECT ON VULNERABILITY

Did you know that fear, anxiety, and uncertainty don't disqualify us from having an impact on others? Rather, in many ways they *qualify* us for leadership and ministry. Particularly as we realize that our reverence for the high calling of God is more important than whatever we fear.

As the apostle Paul said, "When I am weak, then I am strong."

I once shared a message in which I told of a five-month series of crises I endured early in my ministry. It seemed like everything erupted at once in our church: the death of a baby, the molestation of an adolescent by a trusted family friend and church leader, the murder of a key volunteer, and the discovery of immorality deep within the leadership core.

Years later I was speaking to a group and briefly referenced this litany of tragedies from long ago. As soon as I was finished, a business leader immediately came to me.

"Unless a leader has been tested," Mike told me, "I can't really trust him. Now I know that I can trust you."

Our stories of struggle connect us. When we simply share our successes, we are in danger of becoming competitors. When we share our struggles, we become true friends.

READ THE VERSE ON THE OPPOSITE PAGE, THEN REPHRASE AND PERSONALIZE AS A PRAYER FROM YOU TO GOD.

Describe a time you were moved
by someone's personal story.

Do you think of vulnerability as a
strength or a weakness? Expand on
that thought.

When someone is vulnerable with
you, how does it impact your
feelings toward them?

MY "AHA"

Awaken

WHAT PASSAGE OR INSIGHT FELT MOST PERSONAL FOR YOU?

Hear

WHAT MIGHT GOD BE SAYING TO YOU?

Ask

WRITE A PRAYER ASKING GOD TO HELP YOU EMBRACE VULNERABILITY TO BRING BLESSING INTO YOUR LIFE OR INTO THE LIFE OF SOMEONE YOU KNOW.

"

WHAT JOY FOR THOSE
WHOSE RECORD THE LORD
HAS CLEARED OF GUILT,
WHOSE LIVES ARE LIVED IN
COMPLETE HONESTY.

(PSALM 32:2)

"

*David wrote this psalm, very likely after he
sinned with Bathsheba and arranged for her
husband's death.*

REFLECT ON TRUTHFULNESS

Don't underestimate the power of your personal story.

I've heard soul-shaping stories from people who have survived plane crashes, immorality, imprisonment, addictions, bankruptcy, business failures, relationship break-ups, illness, and disillusionment.

What impactful stories have in common is that the people in them came through the other side—the pain they experienced was neither fatal nor final.

In fact, many of the storytellers I've heard have rebounded to greater levels of effectiveness. While they deeply lament their stumbles and failures, they rejoice in how God has leveraged their learnings both for themselves and for others. They've done the hard work of heart work and therefore they are equipped to serve as physicians of the soul. As one leader said, "I regret the things I did for what they were—but not for what they did in me."

Perhaps you are embarrassed by parts of your story. Don't be.

The things we know at the deepest level, the truths that penetrate our hearts and the hearts of others, are not the things we have casually observed, but the things we've learned in the deep cauldron of life's pain.

These are the truths learned through intense suffering and difficulty that have shaped us and that, when shared by us, most help to shape the hearts of others.

READ THE VERSE ON THE OPPOSITE PAGE, THEN REPHRASE AND PERSONALIZE AS A PRAYER FROM YOU TO GOD.

When is the last time you were moved by someone humbly sharing their personal story and how did it inspire you?

How have your stumbles, failures, or wounds humbled you or accomplished something in you?

What truths has suffering made real to you?

MY "AHA"

Awaken

WHAT PASSAGE OR INSIGHT FELT MOST PERSONAL FOR YOU?

Hear

WHAT MIGHT GOD BE SAYING TO YOU?

Ask

WRITE A PRAYER ASKING GOD TO HELP YOU EMBRACE TRUTHFULNESS TO BRING BLESSING INTO YOUR LIFE OR INTO THE LIFE OF SOMEONE YOU KNOW.

JESUS SAID:

NOW YOU ARE MY FRIENDS,
SINCE I HAVE TOLD YOU
EVERYTHING THE FATHER
TOLD ME.

(JOHN 15:15)

REFLECT ON GOING SMALL

One former megachurch pastor is now redefining success.

Greg thought that at the age of fifty-five he would be in a much different place with much more visibility and influence.

Instead, he finds himself serving in a far smaller setting and—much to his surprise—he is more fulfilled than ever.

Greg is discovering the joy of discipling as Jesus did. Jesus never served as lead pastor of a megachurch. Instead, he led a small group. Jesus chose to go deeper with fewer.

Do you long for transformation in your life? Do you want to be a catalyst for transformation in others?

Here's the secret of transformation:

- Go small
- Go slow
- Go strong

This is not a slam against mega churches or those who lead them. I once led one and you may belong to one.

But we can't deny that when Jesus started His redemptive mission, he did not arrange to fill the twelve largest venues in the world. Instead, he chose to invest in twelve followers, instilling in them the gospel and even his own spirit—twelve followers who would go and do the same for others.

READ THE VERSE ON THE OPPOSITE PAGE, THEN REPHRASE AND PERSONALIZE AS A PRAYER FROM YOU TO GOD.

What is your definition of success
in life?

How is your definition of success
different today than when you
were a teenager or young adult?

In a society where "go big or
go home" is the rule of thumb,
describe a time when "going
small" is the wiser approach.

MY "AHA"

A**WAKEN**

WHAT PASSAGE OR INSIGHT FELT MOST PERSONAL FOR YOU?

H**EAR**

WHAT MIGHT GOD BE SAYING TO YOU?

A**SK**

WRITE A PRAYER ASKING GOD TO HELP YOU EMBRACE THE CONCEPT OF GOING SMALL TO BRING BLESSING INTO YOUR LIFE OR INTO THE LIFE OF SOMEONE YOU KNOW.

WE WERE CRUSHED AND
OVERWHELMED BEYOND
OUR ABILITY TO ENDURE,
AND WE THOUGHT WE
WOULD NEVER LIVE
THROUGH IT.

(2 CORINTHIANS 1:8)

*The apostle Paul wrote this after immense
heartache while sharing the Gospel and
launching churches.*

Reflect on Value

Today I no longer lead an impressive and growing ministry reaching thousands. I now work behind the scenes as a sort of undercover pastor. That means I'm no longer in the lead role. Now I'm in a supporting role.

In the process, I'm learning to embrace obscurity and find my fulfillment in personal relationships, not in organizational leadership.

Everyone is valuable to God regardless of performance and status. The gospel compels us to strive, serve and even succeed—not to impress God and others, but because we are loved by God and have already been declared to be of immense value to Him.

Consider when and where you have had the most heart-touching experiences. Almost without exception the most formational experiences occur in the smallest of settings. Our families, our friends, our trusted circles of confidants have shaped us all the most. That's where we feel loved, not for what we do but who we are.

It's in safe community where we discover that we're heart-connected and valued.

Read the verse on the opposite page, then rephrase and personalize as a prayer from you to God.

What do you think God thinks of
you? Are you a burden or a joy to
him? Do your thoughts line up
with Scripture?

With what group of people do you
feel most loved?

Where do you feel that you are
valued? Describe three or more
sources from which you get your
greatest sense of value?

MY "AHA"

WAKEN

WHAT PASSAGE OR INSIGHT FELT MOST PERSONAL FOR YOU?

HEAR

WHAT MIGHT GOD BE SAYING TO YOU?

ASK

WRITE A PRAYER ASKING GOD TO HELP YOU EMBRACE AND DISCOVER YOUR VALUE TO BRING BLESSING INTO YOUR LIFE OR INTO THE LIFE OF SOMEONE YOU KNOW.

SABBATH REFLECTION

Soul work is slow work

WHAT IS DELIGHTING YOU?

WHAT IS DRAINING YOU?

WHAT ARE YOU DISCOVERING?

WHAT ARE YOU DETERMINING TO DO?

WERE ANY OF YOUR ANSWERS INFLUENCED BY YOUR RECENT
READINGS? IF SO, HOW?

2

LIVE HEART-STRONG

Read Chapter 2 from the companion book, Soul Strength: Rhythms for Thriving.

Heart work is hard work.

"My heart needs a surgeon, my soul needs a friend." The words of the Cody Carnes song "Run to the Father" remind me of two of my good friends, one a heart surgeon and the other a neurosurgeon. Their professional skills are unsurpassed, but what has endeared them to so many is that each has a genuine heart of concern.

I've been with each after the post-surgical loss of a patient and seen them wrecked with grief. While they always do their best, their patients don't always do so well. A few don't even survive.

That's when a physician needs a friend, a sort of physician of the soul. We can be that for each other as we remind ourselves and others that the position of savior has been taken. No matter how hard we try, we can be surprised by failure and loss at any time. When those times happen, we need another person to serve as a physician to our soul.

Who has been a "physician of the soul" like that for you?

ENJOY THE FOLLOWING REFLECTIONS:

- ☐ Reflect on Heart Health
- ☐ Reflect on Transparency
- ☐ Reflect on Measuring Up
- ☐ Reflect on Soulish Boldness
- ☐ Reflect on Heart Talk
- ☐ Sabbath Reflection

"

THERE WAS NO REST FOR
US. WE FACED CONFLICT
IN EVERY DIRECTION
. . . BUT GOD, WHO
ENCOURAGES THOSE
WHO ARE DISCOURAGED,
ENCOURAGED US BY THE
ARRIVAL OF TITUS. HIS
PRESENCE WAS A JOY.

(2 CORINTHIANS 7:5-7)

"

REFLECT ON HEART HEALTH

No one can ever be heart healthy alone.

King David wrote in Psalm 138:3: "When I called you answered me, you made me bold and stouthearted" (NIV 1984 edition).

Fundamentally it is God who is the essential source of our heart health and strength; but how does God actually increase our heart health and strength?

He does that through the only two things that are eternal, His Word and His people! We all need others to sharpen, encourage, resource, and connect us.

I think of the verse in the Bible that says, "Two people are better off than one, for they can help each other succeed. If one person falls, the other can reach out and help. But someone who falls alone is in real trouble" (Ecclesiastes 4:9-10).

READ THE VERSE ON THE OPPOSITE PAGE, THEN REPHRASE AND PERSONALIZE AS A PRAYER FROM YOU TO GOD.

How would you assess the health of your heart?

What does "leading from your heart" mean to you?

How do other people and God's Word strengthen who you are in your deepest core?

MY "AHA"

WAKEN

WHAT PASSAGE OR INSIGHT FELT MOST PERSONAL FOR YOU?

H EAR

WHAT MIGHT GOD BE SAYING TO YOU?

A SK

WRITE A PRAYER ASKING GOD TO HELP YOU EMBRACE A GREATER UNDERSTANDING OF HEART HEALTH TO BRING BLESSING INTO YOUR LIFE OR INTO THE LIFE OF SOMEONE YOU KNOW.

"

OH, DEAR CORINTHIAN
FRIENDS! WE HAVE SPOKEN
HONESTLY WITH YOU, AND
OUR HEARTS ARE OPEN TO
YOU. . . . I AM ASKING YOU TO
RESPOND AS IF YOU WERE
MY OWN CHILDREN. OPEN
YOUR HEARTS TO US.

(2 CORINTHIANS 6:11-13)

"

REFLECT ON TRANSPARENCY

Do those closest to you know your heart? Do they know when you're dealing with deep disappointment? Do they know when you're feeling frustrated or hurt, overwhelmed or under supported? Do they know when you are feeling an inner compulsion or conviction; an unshakable passion or a sense of divine determination?

Those closest to us shouldn't have to guess about our feelings, especially in the face of daunting challenges. Candidly sharing our feelings doesn't mean erupting with anger, but at times it does require openly sharing our concerns and heartfelt convictions with passion.

There should always be linkage between our head and our heart. We're called to have both the mind of Christ and also a heart of courage. Sometimes silence isn't golden, it's ungodly! Every godly leader knows that some situations require boldness instead of silence.

READ THE VERSE ON THE OPPOSITE PAGE, THEN REPHRASE AND PERSONALIZE AS A PRAYER FROM YOU TO GOD.

Why do most people hide their
hearts from others? What are
the perceived or real dangers of
transparency?

When you've boldly shared your
heart in the past, what happened?

When you think about revealing
your heart to others, what
emotions does that evoke in you?

MY "AHA"

A**WAKEN**

W**HAT PASSAGE OR INSIGHT FELT MOST PERSONAL FOR YOU?**

H**EAR**

W**HAT MIGHT** G**OD BE SAYING TO YOU?**

A**SK**

W**RITE A PRAYER ASKING** G**OD TO HELP YOU EMBRACE GREATER TRANSPARENCY TO BRING BLESSING INTO YOUR LIFE OR INTO THE LIFE OF SOMEONE YOU KNOW.**

"

WE DO NOT DARE TO
CLASSIFY OR COMPARE
OURSELVES WITH
SOME WHO COMMEND
THEMSELVES. WHEN THEY
MEASURE THEMSELVES
BY THEMSELVES AND
COMPARE THEMSELVES
WITH THEMSELVES, THEY
ARE NOT WISE.

(2 CORINTHIANS 10:12)

Reflect on Measuring Up

When I was younger, I struggled with the question of being good enough. Sometimes I still do, even now that I'm much older. As a skinny, insecure kid growing up in Chicago, I never felt like I quite measured up. I was never good enough to make the high school team, impress all the cute girls, or earn straight A's. Maybe you can relate.

What's worse, I never felt like I measured up in the eyes of God.

Few seem to be content with their level of influence. That's not only true for young college students, but also for seasoned leaders. Not one of the many pastors I know thinks his church is large enough, social media platform popular enough, or influence broad enough.

We live in a world of constant comparison, and we often feel like we just don't measure up.

Clearly, it's not our *performance* for Christ that ultimately matters, but our *position* in Christ. Those of us with a bent toward self-condemnation need to be reminded daily that there is no condemnation for those in Christ.

And as we read in I John 3:20, "If our hearts condemn us . . . God is greater than our hearts."

We all have our limitations. No one is always going to be in first place in every category. This is why we need to hear, ponder and apply the gospel daily. Our standing before God is not a matter of resume but relationship.

READ THE VERSE ON THE OPPOSITE PAGE, THEN REPHRASE AND PERSONALIZE AS A PRAYER FROM YOU TO GOD.

When you compare yourself to
others, what are your thoughts?
What emotions do those thoughts
evoke in you?

Describe an age or experience that
introduced you to the thought that
you don't measure up. Looking
back on that season or event with
the wisdom of hindsight, what
insights do you have?

Describe three or four ways that
performance for Christ differs from
position in Christ.

MY "AHA"

Awaken

WHAT PASSAGE OR INSIGHT FELT MOST PERSONAL FOR YOU?

Hear

WHAT MIGHT GOD BE SAYING TO YOU?

Ask

WRITE A PRAYER ASKING GOD TO HELP YOU EMBRACE YOUR POSITION IN CHRIST OVER PERFORMANCE FOR CHRIST TO BRING BLESSING INTO YOUR LIFE OR INTO THE LIFE OF SOMEONE YOU KNOW.

"

AND I AM CERTAIN THAT
GOD, WHO BEGAN THE
GOOD WORK WITHIN YOU,
WILL CONTINUE HIS WORK
UNTIL IT IS FINALLY FINISHED
ON THE DAY WHEN CHRIST
JESUS RETURNS.

(PHILIPPIANS 1:6)

"

REFLECT ON SOULISH BOLDNESS

Are you more *head strong* or *heart strong*? It's an important question. In a coaching call I was asked to define the difference between head strong and heart strong.

After fumbling around a moment, I suggested that a *head strong leader* approaches challenges with a cocky attitude of *"I've got this!"* By contrast the *heart strong leade*r lives and leads with the humble conviction, *"God's got this!"*

Bravado is *head up*; boldness is *heart up*. Bravado is haughty; boldness is humble. Goliath had bravado; David had boldness.

Incensed that a pagan bully was intimidating the people of God, David's response was not to join the majority cowering in fear, but to stand up with conviction that God would bring victory. Why? David knew that the victory would not be accomplished *by* him, but rather by God *through* him.

David was *heart strong!*

Everything isn't up to you. God is at work! The apostle Paul reminds us that the same power that raised Jesus from the dead is at work in those who believe—and if that doesn't make us strong-hearted, nothing will!

READ THE VERSE ON THE OPPOSITE PAGE, THEN REPHRASE AND PERSONALIZE AS A PRAYER FROM YOU TO GOD.

What does "heart-strong" and
"head-strong" mean to you?

List some ways that your faith in
God nurtures the health of your
heart and soul.

Is your heart hidden from God? Or
does He have your permission to
access your heart and fill you with
boldness? Describe some of the
ways you allow him to do that.

MY "AHA"

WAKEN

WHAT PASSAGE OR INSIGHT FELT MOST PERSONAL FOR YOU?

HEAR

WHAT MIGHT GOD BE SAYING TO YOU?

ASK

WRITE A PRAYER ASKING GOD TO HELP YOU EMBRACE SOULISH BOLDNESS TO BRING BLESSING INTO YOUR LIFE OR INTO THE LIFE OF SOMEONE YOU KNOW.

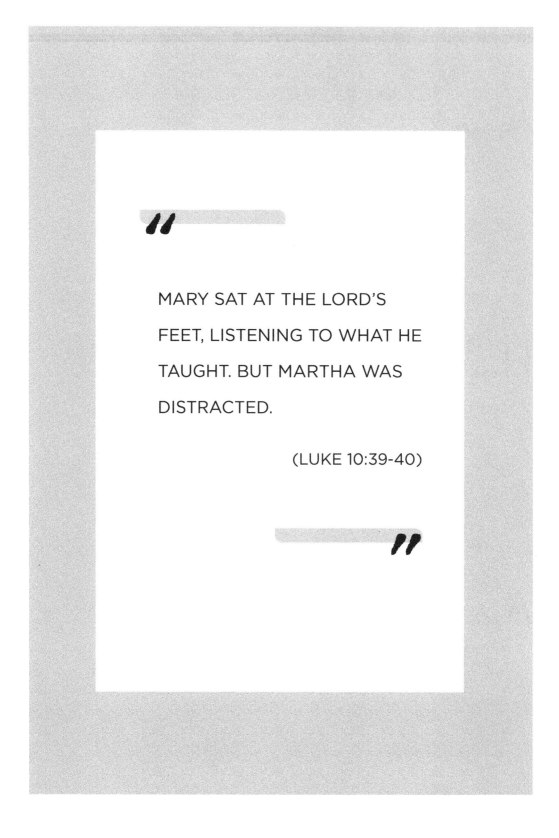

MARY SAT AT THE LORD'S
FEET, LISTENING TO WHAT HE
TAUGHT. BUT MARTHA WAS
DISTRACTED.

(LUKE 10:39-40)

REFLECT ON HEART TALK

"Can you honestly say, 'I have no secrets, and it is well with my soul'?"

I often ask this penetrating question from author Jerry Bridges when with my closest colleagues. Only those who know us best would ever dare ask that question. Who might ask you that question? To whom might you pose that question?

There are three essential ingredients in the recipe for transformational covenant groups:

- Courageous candor
- Humble vulnerability
- Deep non-judgmental listening

"Shop talk" with those who share our faith, politics, interests, or professional pursuits can be a good thing, but a "heady" thing.

By contrast, "soul care" is more of a heart thing, especially focusing on insight, illumination, and transformation.

We all crave community, but rarely experience it. That's because this kind of experience must be intentionally led, sincerely embraced, and fiercely guarded.

READ THE VERSE ON THE OPPOSITE PAGE, THEN REPHRASE AND PERSONALIZE AS A PRAYER FROM YOU TO GOD.

"Can you honestly say, 'I have no secrets, and it is well with my soul'?" Write the names of several people who could ask you that question and receive an honest answer.

What do secrets have to do with the wellness of a soul?

What roles do candor, vulnerability, and non-judgmental listening play in your closest and most intimate group?

MY "AHA"

Awaken

WHAT PASSAGE OR INSIGHT FELT MOST PERSONAL FOR YOU?

Hear

WHAT MIGHT GOD BE SAYING TO YOU?

Ask

WRITE A PRAYER ASKING GOD TO HELP YOU VALUE HEART TALK OVER SHOP TALK TO BRING BLESSING INTO YOUR LIFE OR INTO THE LIFE OF SOMEONE YOU KNOW.

SABBATH REFLECTION

Soul work is slow work

WHAT IS *DELIGHTING* YOU?

WHAT IS *DRAINING* YOU?

WHAT ARE YOU *DISCOVERING*?

WHAT ARE YOU *DETERMINING* TO DO?

WERE ANY OF YOUR ANSWERS INFLUENCED BY YOUR RECENT READINGS? IF SO, HOW?

3

Choose Your Circles

Read Chapter 3 from the companion book, Soul Strength: Rhythms for Thriving.

I met Dr. John Walker shortly after he moved to Colorado to launch Blessing Ranch, a Christian resource and renewal center located in the mountains, more than an hour's drive north of where I lived.

We arranged to meet for lunch, and over our meal I asked, "So, what brings you to town?"

John looked at me with raised eyebrows and gave a surprising one-word answer. "Lunch!"

"Oh! I assumed you had other business in town."

"No," he said, adding, "it gets kind of lonely up there."

That's when we agreed to meet for lunch every month and began talking almost weekly to process the ups and downs of life and ministry.

A long, life-shaping friendship began with one lunch and an innocent question, "So, what brings you to town?"

Life-enriching friendships often begin in unpredictable, even surprising ways. But for that to happen, new friendships must be followed by intentional cultivation. Relational growth is not accidental, it's intentional. We get to choose who we invite and keep in our relational circle for life.

ENJOY THE FOLLOWING REFLECTIONS:

☐ Reflect on Belonging   ☐ Reflect on Toxic People

☐ Reflect on Sacred Allies   ☐ Reflect on Transformation

☐ Reflect on Seats at the Table   ☐ Sabbath Reflection

"

THEREFORE, ACCEPT EACH
OTHER JUST AS CHRIST HAS
ACCEPTED YOU SO THAT
GOD WILL BE GIVEN GLORY.

(ROMANS 15:7)

"

Reflect on Belonging

The missing element in spiritual transformation for many—even for many in Christian leadership—is life with the right people. We all need to encircle ourselves with a core of healthy others who are actively seeking the best for themselves and for us! Both are vital.

We all need partners in soul strength.

How many quality relationships do you enjoy? Sadly, we live in an age of amazing technological connection yet soul-depleting personal disconnection. While many have hundreds of Facebook friends, most have few face-to-face personal friends.

News flash: your life will never be any richer than your relationships! What we know is that good company is catalytic for good outcomes.

In their devotion, *God's Wisdom for Navigating Life*, Tim and Kathy Keller make this point: "In the early stage of your life, you were shaped most by your family. But for the rest of your life, you will be shaped largely by your friends. You become like the people with whom you will spend the most time."

READ THE VERSE ON THE OPPOSITE PAGE, THEN REPHRASE AND PERSONALIZE AS A PRAYER FROM YOU TO GOD.

Q: A:

Do you feel like you belong? To
whom? Who belongs to you?

Q: A:

How have people in your life
shaped you for better or worse?

Q: A:

As you ponder the connection you
have with people on social media
vs face-to-face connections, what
insights can you glean?

MY "AHA"

Awaken

What passage or insight felt most personal for you?

Hear

What might God be saying to you?

Ask

Write a prayer asking God to help you embrace the concept of belonging to bring blessing into your life or into the life of someone you know.

"

I AM FULLY CONVINCED,
MY DEAR BROTHERS AND
SISTERS, THAT YOU ARE FULL
OF GOODNESS. YOU KNOW
THESE THINGS SO WELL, YOU
CAN TEACH EACH OTHER
ALL ABOUT THEM.

(ROMANS 15:14)

"

REFLECT ON SACRED ALLIES

All healthy relationships are for a reason and a season. None will last forever on planet earth. Seasons and circumstances of life are constantly changing.

With that in mind, who are your best friends now, the ones who want something *for* you and not just something *from* you?

Who are your sacred allies? Your soul-enriching friends?

Here are seven clues to help you identify them. Ask yourself:

- Who breathes life into me rather than sucks life out of me?
- Who challenges me spiritually?
- Who sharpens me mentally?
- Who is a friend of my excitement?
- Who makes me laugh?
- Who can keep a confidence?
- Who leaves me feeling more alive?

The point is not to seek to eliminate every difficult person or circumstance in our lives. But we can minimize the soul-stressing impact of toxic people and circumstances by increasing the time we spend with life-giving people and activities.

So, who are the life-giving people in your life? What are the lifegiving activities in which you engage?

READ THE VERSE ON THE OPPOSITE PAGE, THEN REPHRASE AND PERSONALIZE AS A PRAYER FROM YOU TO GOD.

Who are your sacred allies, friends
who want something for you and
not just from you?

Ask God for wisdom about a
relationship that feels draining or
even toxic. What do you think He
might be saying to you?

What would you have to do to
engage with one life-giving friend
or activity every day? How might
your life feel different if you could
make that happen?

MY "AHA"

Awaken

WHAT PASSAGE OR INSIGHT FELT MOST PERSONAL FOR YOU?

Hear

WHAT MIGHT GOD BE SAYING TO YOU?

Ask

WRITE A PRAYER ASKING GOD TO HELP YOU EMBRACE THE IDEA OF SACRED ALLIES TO BRING BLESSING INTO YOUR LIFE OR INTO THE LIFE OF SOMEONE YOU KNOW.

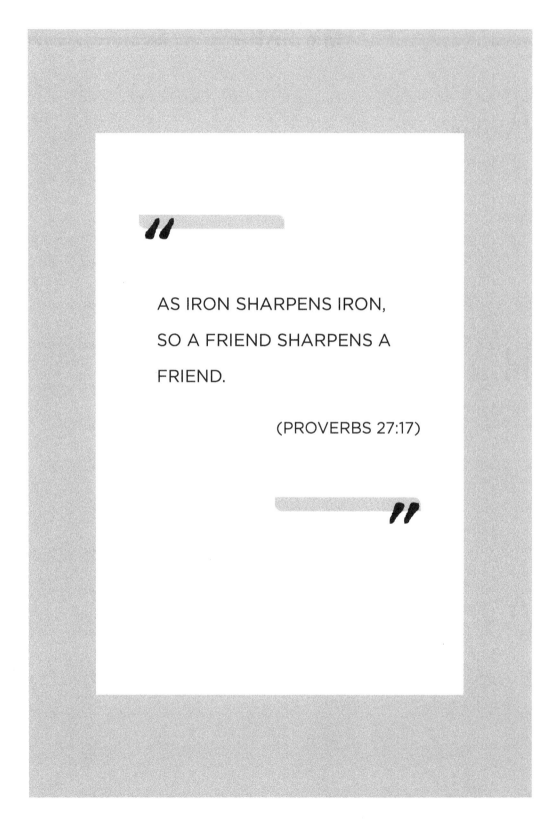

AS IRON SHARPENS IRON,
SO A FRIEND SHARPENS A
FRIEND.

(PROVERBS 27:17)

REFLECT ON SEATS AT THE TABLE

We all need to sit in a circle of trust with those who love us and respect us, but aren't always impressed by us!

Who sits in the circle at your table? They may not know each other, but they know you and play a vital role in your life. Some may shift seats or even enjoy more than one of the four important seats:

- **The Work Chair:** People who sharpen you, inspiring you to improve your efficiency and your effectiveness. *"As iron sharpens iron, so one man sharpens another"* (Proverbs 27:17 NIV). *Who sharpens you?*

- **The Wisdom Chair:** People who deepen you by asking uncommon questions and modeling uncommon candor. They may or may not be the smartest people at your table, but they're likely to be among the most curious and honest. *Who deepens you?*

- **The Well-Being Chair:** People who demonstrate a pattern of happily enriching, blessing, and uplifting you. They may share their resources, but even more, their hearts, homes and even their good humor. *Who enriches you?*

- **The WOO Chair:** This is an abbreviation for "winning others over" and represents those who connect you with others. Friends love to introduce their friends to the friends who open up opportunities for them. *Who connects you?*

Read the verse on the opposite page, then rephrase and personalize as a prayer from you to God.

Who is in each of these "chairs" in
your circle, and why?
Work:
Wisdom:
Well-being:
WOO

When have you last spent
unhurried time with each of these
people?

Do these people know how
influential they are to you? If not,
how could you best tell them?

MY "AHA"

A**WAKEN**

W**HAT PASSAGE OR INSIGHT FELT MOST PERSONAL FOR YOU?**

H**EAR**

W**HAT MIGHT** G**OD BE SAYING TO YOU?**

A**SK**

W**RITE A PRAYER ASKING** G**OD TO HELP YOU FILL THE** "**SEATS AT YOUR TABLE**" **WISELY IN ORDER TO BRING BLESSING INTO YOUR LIFE OR INTO THE LIFE OF SOMEONE YOU KNOW.**

"

IF PEOPLE ARE CAUSING
DIVISIONS AMONG YOU,
GIVE A FIRST AND SECOND
WARNING. AFTER THAT,
HAVE NOTHING MORE TO DO
WITH THEM.

(TITUS 3:10)

"

REFLECT ON TOXIC PEOPLE

We all know people who are not life-givers to us but life-suckers. They leave us feeling drained or angry or sad. When we are with them, we know we are not the best version of ourselves. And if they bring out the worst in us, we're probably not bringing out the best in them.

Dr. John Walker once said he determined not to invest undue time placating or befriending a toxic person. The reality is that toxic people with toxic attitudes not only abound, but they also surround us all. That's at least true via our technology, if not in our actual community.

The key is to minimize those influences by maximizing the life-giving influences of those who bring the best to us and seek the best for us.

On the other hand, no one can or should strive to avoid *every* challenging person or situation. Oswald Chambers said, "I feel sorry for the Christian who doesn't have something in the circumstances of his life that he wishes were not there." And he has a point—these are often the people and events through which we experience great growth.

At the same time, it's best that we identify these people so we can manage the experience. How can we manage toxic people in our lives? Pray for them. Limit time together. Ask God for wisdom. Compensate for the drain with life-giving people. Ask God to help you know when to leave that person to him and move on.

Read the verse on the opposite page, then rephrase and personalize as a prayer from you to God.

What physical or emotional signs
have you recognized in yourself
that help you realize when
someone is toxic or draining to
you?

Can you think of stories or
instructions in the Bible that give
us any guidance on how to deal
with difficult people?

Is there ever a time to eliminate
toxic people from our lives? If so,
when?

MY "AHA"

Awaken

What passage or insight felt most personal for you?

Hear

What might God be saying to you?

Ask

Write a prayer asking God to help you deal wisely with toxic people in order to bring blessing into your life or into the life of someone you know.

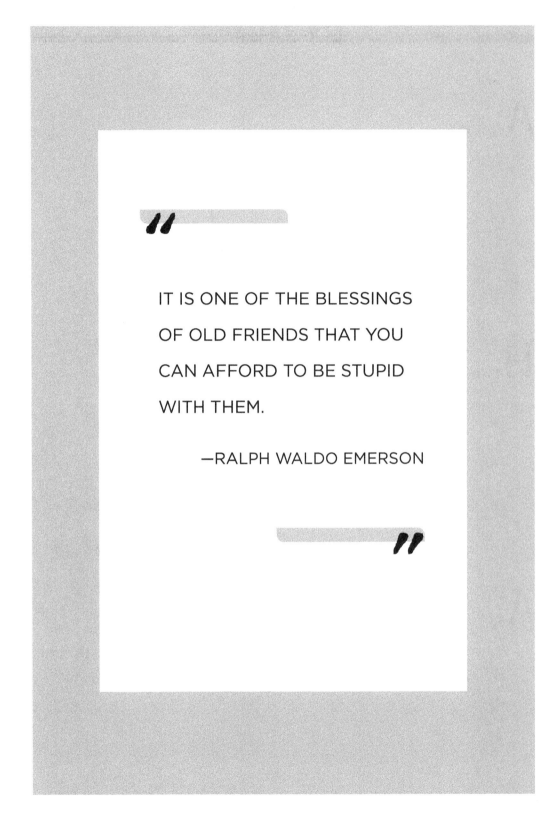

"

IT IS ONE OF THE BLESSINGS
OF OLD FRIENDS THAT YOU
CAN AFFORD TO BE STUPID
WITH THEM.

—RALPH WALDO EMERSON

"

REFLECT ON TRANSFORMATION

Some attribute transformation and growth to the formula:

Change of Place + Change of Pace = Change of Perspective.

I love that, but I would suggest one more element. Change of perspective almost always happens in community—that is, with other people who sharpen and deepen us.

Change of Place + Pace + PEOPLE = Change in Perspective

Change of Place involves an actual location. That might be a vacation getaway, your favorite coffee shop or simply the leather recliner in your own home.

Change of Pace involves deliberately choosing to be still. Most of us allow our days to be filled with noise from beginning to end. Whenever I lead one of our Covenant Group retreats, we regularly "take two." That's the simple discipline of periodically enjoying two minutes of silence.

Change of People involves allowing yourself to enter the inner world of others and allow them to enter your own. And that requires courage. As Brené Brown has written, the prefix "cor" of our English word *courage* springs from the Latin word that means speaking one's mind by sharing all of one's heart. Few of us need to be surrounded by more people, we need to encircle ourselves with the *right* people.

R EAD THE QUOTE ON THE OPPOSITE PAGE, THEN REPHRASE AND PERSONALIZE AS A PRAYER FROM YOU TO GOD.

Describe a time when a change
of place or pace gave you a whole
new perspective.

What might a "change of people"
look like in your life?

Are you encircling yourself with
the right people? If yes, why are
they the right people? If no, what
can you do about it?

MY "AHA"

Awaken

WHAT PASSAGE OR INSIGHT FELT MOST PERSONAL FOR YOU?

Hear

WHAT MIGHT GOD BE SAYING TO YOU?

Ask

WRITE A PRAYER ASKING GOD TO HELP YOU EMBRACE THE KEY TO TRANSFORMATION TO BRING BLESSING INTO YOUR LIFE OR INTO THE LIFE OF SOMEONE YOU KNOW.

SABBATH REFLECTION

Soul work is slow work

WHAT IS *DELIGHTING* YOU?

WHAT IS *DRAINING* YOU?

WHAT ARE YOU *DISCOVERING*?

WHAT ARE YOU *DETERMINING* TO DO?

WERE ANY OF YOUR ANSWERS INFLUENCED BY YOUR RECENT READINGS? IF SO, HOW?

4

Cultivate Strong Relationships

Read Chapter 4 from the companion book, Soul Strength: Rhythms for Thriving.

During a season of high stress and deep disappointment, I hesitantly shared a heartbreak with a close friend over lunch.

I was stunned when my business buddy suddenly looked me in the eye and said urgently, "You are under attack, I need to pray for you!"

Right there, in the booth of the Italian restaurant, he grabbed both of my hands and shared a heartfelt passionate prayer. I've never had a business guy so boldly turn pastor on me like that!

Even though that happened years ago, I've never forgotten it.

Close friends and strong relationships are worth their weight in gold. But friendships like that don't happen by accident—they require five areas of investment: authenticity, devotion, intentionality, time, and cultivation.

ENJOY THE FOLLOWING REFLECTIONS:

☐ Reflect on Authenticity   ☐ Reflect on Time

☐ Reflect on Devotion   ☐ Reflect on Cultivation

☐ Reflect on Intentionality   ☐ Sabbath Reflection

IF WE DON'T MAKE TIME FOR
FRIENDS, WE WON'T HAVE
ANY.

—RABBI FROM *THE CHOSEN*

Reflect on Authenticity

Have you ever broken someone's trust? Has someone broken yours?

We all take turns letting people down. Sometimes it's just an inadvertent oversight, other times it might be a matter of deliberate betrayal. Imperfections are inevitable. However, there's a big difference between the relational stress that comes from a simple oversight such as, "Oops I forgot to return your call!" and an entrenched pattern of self-protection or deceit.

Most of us have learned the hard way that broken relationships are rebuilt slowly.

Trust must be earned. As King David wrote, "I will search for faithful people to be my companions" (Psalm 101:6).

Five years ago, I was in a covenant group that soon went deep. While we all knew each other prior, our relationships grew far beyond anything we had experienced together before. They reached the point where we had no secrets.

We breathed the rare air of trust. One of the guys closed our three-year soul care journey by saying, "I can't believe it took me well into my sixties to finally experience something like this!"

It's never too soon to begin building relationships of trust. And it's worth the investment to begin again if trust has been broken.

READ THE QUOTE ON THE OPPOSITE PAGE, THEN REPHRASE AND PERSONALIZE AS A PRAYER FROM YOU TO GOD.

Why is authenticity foundational to
trust?

Has someone rebuilt broken trust
with you? Or you with them? What
did it take? What factors were
most influential in reestablishing
trust?

What roles do unforgiveness and
boundaries play in rebuilding
broken trust?

MY "AHA"

Awaken

WHAT PASSAGE OR INSIGHT FELT MOST PERSONAL FOR YOU?

Hear

WHAT MIGHT GOD BE SAYING TO YOU?

Ask

WRITE A PRAYER ASKING GOD TO HELP YOU VALUE AND PRACTICE AUTHENTICITY TO BRING BLESSING INTO YOUR LIFE OR INTO THE LIFE OF SOMEONE YOU KNOW.

"

THESE PEOPLE LEFT OUR
CHURCHES, BUT THEY NEVER
REALLY BELONGED WITH US;
OTHERWISE THEY WOULD
HAVE STAYED WITH US.
WHEN THEY LEFT, IT PROVED
THAT THEY DID NOT BELONG
WITH US.

(1 JOHN 2:19)

"

REFLECT ON DEVOTION

One of the keys to understanding the community of the early church is an often-overlooked word in our culture. The word is *devoted*. In our culture few are devoted to much of anything or anyone beyond themselves. We see that in the mobility of the culture at large, the breakdown of the family, the disintegration of communities and even the lack of loyalty to local congregations.

In Greek, the word *koinonia* means community. The Father, Son and Spirit were in perfect community before the beginning of time. We have been redeemed to enjoy community with the Lord and His people for both time and eternity.

This is why the phrase "one another" appears 59 times in the Scripture. Here are a few examples:

- Love one another (I John 3:11).
- Instruct one another (Romans 15:14 NIV).
- Encourage one another (I Thessalonians 5:11 NIV).
- Spur one another towards love and good deeds (Hebrews 10:24 NIV).
- Rejoice and weep with one another (Romans 12:15 NET).
- Forgive one another (Ephesians 4:32).
- Confess our sins to one another (James 5:16 NET).
- Pray for one another (James 5:16 NET)

Clearly, we are better together. We belong together as partners with Christ and with one another.

READ THE VERSE ON THE OPPOSITE PAGE, THEN REPHRASE AND PERSONALIZE AS A PRAYER FROM YOU TO GOD.

What are the pros and cons of
"church hopping"?

What does the word devotion mean
to you?

How does our disposable society
impact our concept of loyalty and
devotion?

MY "AHA"

Awaken

WHAT PASSAGE OR INSIGHT FELT MOST PERSONAL FOR YOU?

Hear

WHAT MIGHT GOD BE SAYING TO YOU?

Ask

WRITE A PRAYER ASKING GOD TO HELP YOU PRACTICE DEVOTION IN YOUR RELATIONSHIPS TO BRING BLESSING INTO YOUR LIFE OR INTO THE LIFE OF SOMEONE YOU KNOW.

"

DEEP FRIENDSHIPS CAN
BEGIN SUDDENLY AND
UNEXPECTEDLY, BUT THEY
CAN ONLY ENDURE IF
THEY ARE CULTIVATED
INTENTIONALLY.

—ALAN AHLGRIM

"

REFLECT ON INTENTIONALITY

David Benner has written a profound book entitled *Sacred Companions: The Gift of Spiritual Friendship & Direction*. In it he writes, "The hunger for connection is one of the most fundamental desires of the human heart.... In the core of our being we yearn for intimacy. We want people to share our lives. We want soul friends.... Paradoxically, however, what we most deeply long for we also fear."

Everyone agrees that cultivating these kinds of deep relationships is vital; therefore, most plan to do it . . . *next year*. My mission is to challenge them to make *next year* happen *this year*!

Here's what we know from decades of church programming. Church programs don't produce transformation. Here's what we know from the model of Jesus. Transformation happens on purpose, over time, and in community.

Soul-enriching connections can't happen soon enough. We all need a vital few that know us well.

And we need them now.

Healthy and fulfilling relationships are too important to be left to chance because they are essential to a healthy and fulfilling life.

What investment are you making in your healthy and fulfilling life?

Read the quote on the opposite page, then rephrase and personalize as a prayer from you to God.

How intentional are you about
nurturing authentic connection
with others?

What action can you take today to
nurture an existing connection or
explore a new one?

Who do you know who might be
ready and willing to enrich you
and to be enriched by you?

MY "AHA"

Awaken

WHAT PASSAGE OR INSIGHT FELT MOST PERSONAL FOR YOU?

Hear

WHAT MIGHT GOD BE SAYING TO YOU?

Ask

WRITE A PRAYER ASKING GOD TO HELP YOU MAKE INTENTIONAL IN-VESTMENTS IN RELATIONSHIPS TO BRING BLESSING INTO YOUR LIFE OR INTO THE LIFE OF SOMEONE YOU KNOW.

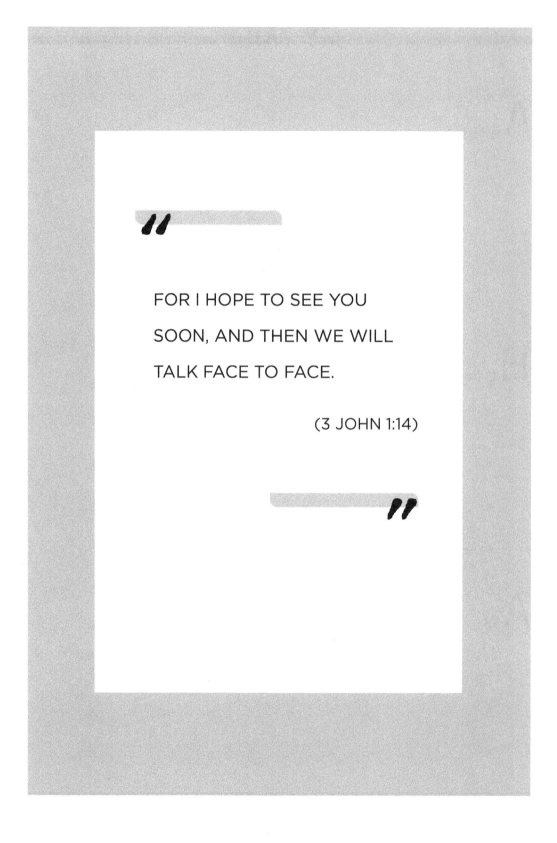

FOR I HOPE TO SEE YOU
SOON, AND THEN WE WILL
TALK FACE TO FACE.

(3 JOHN 1:14)

REFLECT ON TIME

Many years ago Samuel Chadwick wrote: "Hurry is the death of prayer." To that I would add, "Hurry is the death of depth."

When was the last time that you enjoyed a relaxed and unhurried face-to-face conversation with someone you value and trust? Often when I ask this question, I see a bit of sadness sweep across a face as the person comes to grips with the dearth of heartfelt and soul-enriching relationships in their life.

During the Covid closures countless gatherings were cancelled. One leader told me, "I told my wife I'm not sure I can handle another year merely connecting via Zoom. I miss being with people!"

It's the same cry of the heart we've all sensed and heard many times. Loneliness is epidemic but it can be cured through deep connection. Lingering conversations are essential for life transformation and relational fulfillment.

READ THE VERSE ON THE OPPOSITE PAGE, THEN PERSONALIZE IT IN YOUR OWN WORDS AS A PRAYER FROM YOU TO GOD

Where do you invest more of your time? Your phone? Computer? Social media? People you say are important in your life?

What impact do you think phones and devices are having on the scarcity of deep lingering conversations with people in our lives?

What action can you take to enjoy more hurry-free, distraction-free conversations with people in your life?

MY "AHA"

Awaken

WHAT PASSAGE OR INSIGHT FELT MOST PERSONAL FOR YOU?

Hear

WHAT MIGHT GOD BE SAYING TO YOU?

Ask

WRITE A PRAYER ASKING GOD TO HELP YOU ENGAGE IN MORE LINGERING, SOUL-ENRICHING CONVERSATIONS TO BRING BLESSING INTO YOUR LIFE OR INTO THE LIFE OF SOMEONE YOU KNOW.

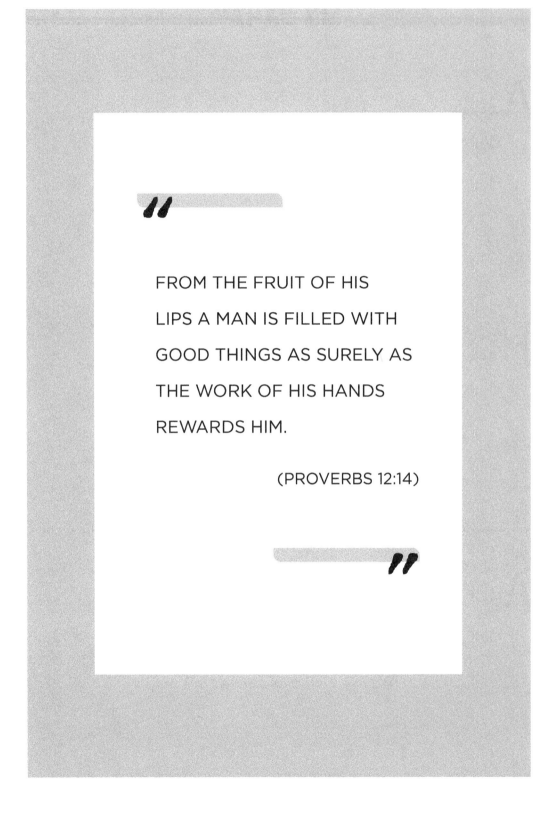

"

FROM THE FRUIT OF HIS

LIPS A MAN IS FILLED WITH

GOOD THINGS AS SURELY AS

THE WORK OF HIS HANDS

REWARDS HIM.

(PROVERBS 12:14)

"

Reflect on Cultivation

Questions are a powerful tool for cultivating depth in your relationships.

Questions do more than give you information about your friend or family member—they help your friend or family member feel known by you, and that cultivates a deeper connection.

Try a few of these in your next hurry-free, distraction-free conversation with someone in your life:

- If you were to die this evening with no opportunity to communicate with anyone, what would you most regret not having told someone? Why haven't you told them yet?
- What is your most treasured memory?
- What is your most terrible memory?
- Given the choice of anyone in the world, whom would you want as a dinner guest?

READ THE VERSE ON THE OPPOSITE PAGE, THEN REPHRASE AND PERSONALIZE AS A PRAYER FROM YOU TO GOD.

The temptation will be to ask a
question and then move on to
another topic or question without
asking follow-ups or allowing time
to linger on the topic. Don't be in
a rush! From 1 to 10 (10 being
GREAT!) how good of a listener are
you?

Describe how it makes you feel
when someone asks questions
about your life and is genuinely
interested in your answers.

Besides asking questions,
how else might you cultivate
connection?

MY "AHA"

Awaken

What passage or insight felt most personal for you?

Hear

What might God be saying to you?

Ask

Write a prayer asking God to help you ask questions to cultivate deeper relationships in order to bring blessing into your life or into the life of someone you know.

SABBATH REFLECTION

Soul work is slow work

WHAT IS *DELIGHTING* YOU?

WHAT IS *DRAINING* YOU?

WHAT ARE YOU *DISCOVERING*?

WHAT ARE YOU *DETERMINING* TO DO?

WERE ANY OF YOUR ANSWERS INFLUENCED BY YOUR RECENT
READINGS? IF SO, HOW?

5

Learn the Rhythms of Grace

Read Chapter 5 from the companion book, Soul Strength: Rhythms for Thriving.

"You're driving me crazy! Slow down. Everything doesn't have to be finished before we leave town!"

Those challenging words were spoken to me by Linda, my wife for life.

And she was right. In my frantic rush to accomplish last-minute chores before a trip, I was making too many things a top priority all at the same time. Sometimes when I'm under stress I'm not the best version of me. Linda uses a highly technical term for that. She calls it my "wacko condition."

While I'm usually an easygoing and happy life partner, I'm not always calm and laid back.

When I am under stress, every minor issue becomes urgent. I used to think that I was an amazing multitasker. Now I realize that I have actually been a hyper-active multi-switcher.

That's when I need to take a breath. Literally. I need to be reminded again that by God's grace I have all the time I need to do everything He wants me to do!

ENJOY THE FOLLOWING REFLECTIONS:

- [ ] Reflect on People-Pleasing
- [ ] Reflect on Boulders
- [ ] Reflect on Stress
- [ ] Reflect on Grace
- [ ] Reflect on Rhythms
- [ ] Sabbath Reflection

"

OBVIOUSLY, I'M NOT TRYING
TO WIN THE APPROVAL OF
PEOPLE, BUT OF GOD. IF
PLEASING PEOPLE WERE
MY GOAL, I WOULD NOT BE
CHRIST'S SERVANT.

(GALATIANS 1:10)

"

REFLECT ON PEOPLE-PLEASING

I have been an acceptance addict, and I've paid a high price. The desire for acceptance has at times driven me to ridiculous levels of performance through people-pleasing and approval seeking. I didn't want to disappoint anyone. I wanted everyone to be happy with me and admire my efforts to serve them and others. I even sacrificed my family, free time, and health in the service of others.

I have approached God this way as well. For too many years I have been driven and burdened in my pursuit of God and doing God's will. Will He love me? Will He approve of me?

Some years ago, I received an award along with the gift of a beautiful item made of marble and crystal. It depicted a man pushing a huge boulder up a steep hill.

Many of you will recall the Greek myth of Sisyphus and how he was condemned to push a boulder up a hill. Each time he got near the top the boulder came rolling back down the hill again.

As soon as I opened the box and saw the figure, it resonated with me. That's how I felt. I had to keep pushing the heavy burdens of life or else they would crush me. I couldn't cease. I couldn't stop. I couldn't relax. I had to keep pushing.

The boulder for me was the unrelenting pressure to perform. As a result of the boulder, I often blamed myself for not being good enough or working hard enough. I even blamed my wife and a few others for not understanding me or supporting me enough. Ultimately, I blamed God for giving me such a heavy burden to push.

READ THE VERSE ON THE OPPOSITE PAGE, THEN REPHRASE AND PERSONALIZE AS A PRAYER FROM YOU TO GOD.

Do you think those who have more
people-pleasing tendencies are
more respected by others?

Does your need for love and
acceptance feel like a burden?

Does your need to perform feel
like a burden? If you do not
perform well, what does that mean
to you?

MY "AHA"

Awaken

WHAT PASSAGE OR INSIGHT FELT MOST PERSONAL FOR YOU?

Hear

WHAT MIGHT GOD BE SAYING TO YOU?

Ask

WRITE A PRAYER ASKING GOD TO HELP YOU ADDRESS ANY PEOPLE-PLEASING TENDANCIES YOU MAY HAVE, IN ORDER TO BRING BLESSING INTO YOUR LIFE OR INTO THE LIFE OF SOMEONE YOU KNOW.

"

I HAVE WORKED HARD AND
LONG, ENDURING MANY
SLEEPLESS NIGHTS. I HAVE
BEEN HUNGRY AND THIRSTY
AND HAVE OFTEN GONE
WITHOUT FOOD. . . BESIDES
ALL THIS, I HAVE THE DAILY
BURDEN OF MY CONCERN
FOR ALL THE CHURCHES.

(2 CORINTHIANS 11:27-28)

"

Reflect on Boulders

Every leader feels at times that they are pushing something uphill. Those who score as "achievers" on the Enneagram personality profile especially resonate with this.

One of my close friends is a wealth manager. He shared how his "performance boulder" represents a couple of hundred investment portfolios that he manages for his clients. He daily lives with the angst that if he advises everyone to stay in the market when it dives his clients could take a beating. On the other hand, if he cautiously advises his clients to take a conservative approach and hold heavy cash positions when the market soars, he fails them.

After Dave shared this picture with his wife, Angela, she said, "Well, Dave, my portfolio is the welfare of our daughters. If they're not doing well, I'm not doing well!"

Everyone has some sort of portfolio of concern. Everyone has a boulder of some sort they are pushing.

What's yours?

READ THE VERSE ON THE OPPOSITE PAGE, THEN REPHRASE AND PERSONALIZE AS A PRAYER FROM YOU TO GOD.

What is your boulder and how
might you best label it?

What experiences, losses, or
trauma in your past might be
fueling an excessive need for love
and acceptance from God and
other people?

What keeps you from saying "no"
to the burdens you have placed on
yourself or received from others?

MY "AHA"

A**WAKEN**

W**HAT PASSAGE OR INSIGHT FELT MOST PERSONAL FOR YOU?**

H**EAR**

W**HAT MIGHT** G**OD BE SAYING TO YOU?**

A**SK**

W**RITE A PRAYER ASKING** G**OD TO HELP YOU IDENTIFY THE BOULDERS THAT ARE CAUSING YOU STRESS, IN ORDER TO BRING BLESSING INTO YOUR LIFE OR INTO THE LIFE OF SOMEONE YOU KNOW.**

"

SO TO KEEP ME FROM
BECOMING PROUD, I WAS
GIVEN A THORN IN MY
FLESH, A MESSENGER FROM
SATAN TO TORMENT ME AND
KEEP ME FROM BECOMING
PROUD.

(2 CORINTHIANS 12:7)

"

REFLECT ON STRESS

While people like me may get a lot done and take pride in the doing of it, in our relentless pushing we often lose our footing. Pushing ourselves leads to personal burnout. Pushing others leads to relational breakdowns. I know about both.

I just couldn't stop achieving more or worrying that I wasn't.

At one point my physician challenged me.

He said, "When are you going to do something about the stress you are carrying? This isn't good for you!"

Not long after that, I was diagnosed with a stress fracture. My wife insisted that I get a bone density test. The doctors discovered that I had severe osteoporosis in much of my body. Do you know who typically gets that? Heavy smokers, drinkers, and post-menopausal octogenarians!

I was none of the above. However, I later learned from the book, *The Heartmath Solution,* that the stress hormone cortisol depletes calcium from the bones and is a precursor to osteoporosis.

At that point, I became convicted. For years, when it came to stress, I prided myself on being a *power lifter*. Many wondered how I carried so much responsibility so well. Frankly, so did I. I wondered how I was getting away with my addiction to performance.

Well, I didn't get away with it.

And neither can you.

READ THE VERSE ON THE OPPOSITE PAGE, THEN REPHRASE AND PERSONALIZE AS A PRAYER FROM YOU TO GOD.

On a scale of one to ten, how
stressed do you feel in an average
day?

What impact is stress having on
your emotions? Your body? Your
soul?

What impact is stress having on
your relationships, with God and
with other people in your life?

MY "AHA"

Awaken

WHAT PASSAGE OR INSIGHT FELT MOST PERSONAL FOR YOU?

Hear

WHAT MIGHT GOD BE SAYING TO YOU?

Ask

WRITE A PRAYER ASKING GOD TO HELP YOU IDENTIFY AND ADDRESS STRESS IN ORDER TO BRING BLESSING INTO YOUR LIFE OR INTO THE LIFE OF SOMEONE YOU KNOW.

> **"**
>
> IT WAS OUR SORROWS THAT WEIGHED HIM DOWN. . . . HE WAS PIERCED FOR OUR REBELLION, CRUSHED FOR OUR SINS. HE WAS BEATEN SO WE COULD BE MADE WHOLE. HE WAS WHIPPED SO WE COULD BE HEALED.
>
> (ISAIAH 53:4-5)
>
> **"**

REFLECT ON GRACE

My "performance boulder" and approval addiction was driven home for me at a men's retreat a few years ago. I had no idea what I was getting into when shortly after I arrived one of the hosts privately interviewed me, asking a soul-searching question.

"What do you want to work on while you are here?"

"I want to feel more of the love and acceptance of God," I blurted. My words, though true, sounded immature and needy, especially for a sixty-six-year-old long-time Christian leader.

After my new friends heard some of my story, they surprised me with an intervention. I was blindfolded and carefully laid on what I quickly realized was a large wooden cross. One by one, stones were placed on my back. With each of the stones some of my own performance words were used. As the stones piled up, my emotions did as well. Suddenly I was heaving with tears, sobbing uncontrollably with snot flowing freely.

The wise men standing around and over me let my emotions run their course. Then each took a turn removing the stones. As they did, they blessed me with liberating words of acceptance.

They repeatedly reminded me of the grace of Jesus and His acceptance of me—an acceptance not based on my performance but on His!

After that experience on the floor, I have often worn a crucifix. I once thought it was almost heretical for good Protestant kids like me to revere a crucifix. After all, we don't worship a dead hero but a living Lord! That's certainly true; however, now the crucifix reminds me that the position of Savior has been taken!

I understand at a deeper level than ever that I am loved apart from what I do. I am accepted apart from how I perform. I am forgiven and blame free apart from anything I deserve. And it's all because of what Christ has done for me.

READ THE VERSE ON THE OPPOSITE PAGE, THEN REPHRASE AND PERSONALIZE AS A PRAYER FROM YOU TO GOD.

Where does your boulder come from? Do you take it on yourself, or has it been laid upon you by others?

Q:

How might it change your life if you truly believed you were loved apart from what you do?

Q:

Jesus' death on the cross means your value is not tied to your performance. Write a letter thanking Him for His sacrifice and exploring what that gift means to you.

MY "AHA"

Awaken

WHAT PASSAGE OR INSIGHT FELT MOST PERSONAL FOR YOU?

Hear

WHAT MIGHT GOD BE SAYING TO YOU?

Ask

WRITE A PRAYER ASKING GOD TO HELP YOU EMBRACE GRACE TO BRING BLESSING INTO YOUR LIFE OR INTO THE LIFE OF SOMEONE YOU KNOW.

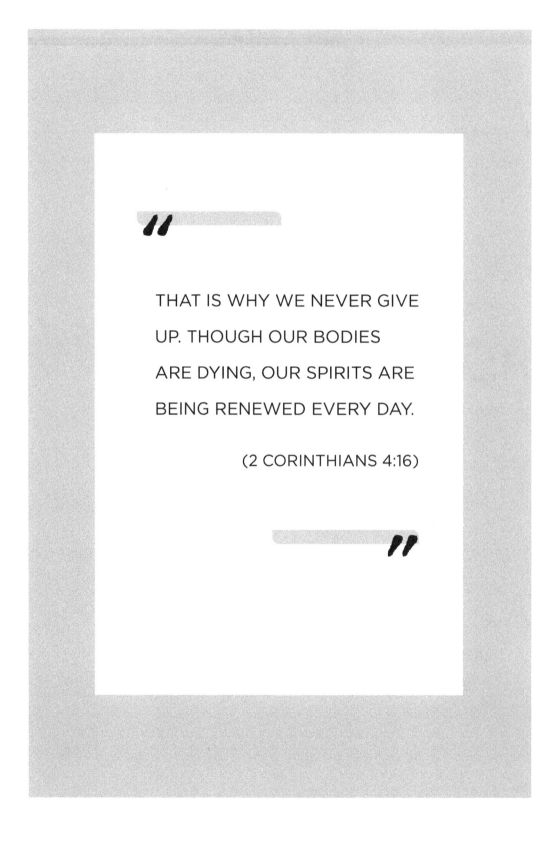

THAT IS WHY WE NEVER GIVE
UP. THOUGH OUR BODIES
ARE DYING, OUR SPIRITS ARE
BEING RENEWED EVERY DAY.

(2 CORINTHIANS 4:16)

Reflect on Rhythms

"Are you tired? Worn out? Burned out on religion? Come to me. Get away with me and you'll recover your life. I'll show you how to take a real rest. Walk with me and work with me. Watch how I do it. Learn the unforced rhythms of grace. I won't lay anything heavy or ill-fitting on you. Keep company with me and you'll learn to live freely and lightly" (Matthew 11:28-30, The Message).

I'm discovering that just as my life will never be richer than my relationships, my life will never be richer than my rhythms! Jesus invites us to rest, recover, walk with Him, work with Him, watch Him. He invites us to learn to live freely and lightly.

These are the unforced rhythms of grace.

I've learned how to embrace life-giving rhythms in three areas: reflectively, relationally, and recreationally.

- My *reflective rhythms* ground me in God's daily mercies. I love to begin each day slowly soaking in God's Word and presence, listening for His leading, and seeking His prompting.
- My *relational rhythms* connect me with the gift of disciplined community. I daily seek to connect with life-enhancing people that sharpen, deepen, resource, and connect me.
- My *recreational rhythms* invigorate me in body, mind, and spirit with God's creation. Daily exercise isn't an interruption in my life, it's an enhancement.

King David once prayed, "The LORD be exalted, who delights in the well-being of his servant" (Psalm 35:27 NIV).

Thriving is all about well-being. Frankly, too many times my "stinkin' thinkin'" and substandard theology has led me to patterns that were far from conducive to my wellbeing.

Read the verse on the opposite page, then rephrase and personalize as a prayer from you to God.

Describe what this phrase means to you: "If you don't feel as close to God as you once did, guess who moved?" (See James 4:8.)

What helps you get out from behind the boulder? What helps you thrive in His love and grace?

What daily rhythms do you practice that leave you revitalized instead of drained? If you can't think of any, make a list of rhythms with which you can experiment. Which one will you practice today?

MY "AHA"

Awaken

WHAT PASSAGE OR INSIGHT FELT MOST PERSONAL FOR YOU?

Hear

WHAT MIGHT GOD BE SAYING TO YOU?

Ask

WRITE A PRAYER ASKING GOD TO HELP YOU EMBRACE HEALTHIER RHYTHMS IN ORDER TO BRING BLESSING INTO YOUR LIFE OR INTO THE LIFE OF SOMEONE YOU KNOW.

SABBATH REFLECTION
Soul work is slow work

WHAT IS *DELIGHTING* YOU?

WHAT IS *DRAINING* YOU?

WHAT ARE YOU *DISCOVERING*?

WHAT ARE YOU *DETERMINING* TO DO?

WERE ANY OF YOUR ANSWERS INFLUENCED BY YOUR RECENT READINGS? IF SO, HOW?

6

CHOOSE PURITY

Read Chapter 6 from the companion book, Soul Strength: Rhythms for Thriving.

A decade ago, a young doctor I know well (who happens to be my son) reported that several medical colleagues of his had lost their reputations, medical licenses, and military careers because of sexual misconduct.

Then he shared with me what he does in his practice to avoid trouble. "When examining a female patient, we *always* have a female assistant in the room. The other thing I personally do is to narrate everything I do. This keeps the patient more relaxed since they know what I am looking for and why. It also keeps my mind on the task. If you are doing verbal patient education along the way, you're staying very focused—therefore, your thoughts never can wander."

Temptation is inescapable and always presents us with a choice. We can choose to escape it, endure it successfully, or succumb to it. Technically speaking, no one "falls into sin." We either step into it or step away from it.

ENJOY THE FOLLOWING REFLECTIONS:

☐ Reflect on Vulnerability to Sin   ☐ Reflect on Accountability

☐ Reflect on Our Enemy   ☐ Reflect on the 4 Ds

☐ Reflect on Sexual Temptation   ☐ Sabbath Reflection

"

AND LET US CONSIDER HOW
WE MAY SPUR ONE ANOTHER
ON TOWARD LOVE AND
GOOD DEEDS, NOT GIVING
UP MEETING TOGETHER, AS
SOME ARE IN THE HABIT OF
DOING, BUT ENCOURAGING
ONE ANOTHER.

(HEBREWS 10:24-25 NIV)

"

REFLECT ON VULNERABILITY TO SIN

In recent days we have been stunned with tragic stories of exceptionally gifted Christian leaders who crashed and burned. They had enjoyed exceptional gifts and freedoms, but they abused them. They brought shame to themselves, their families, and their ministries.

The truth is, no one is exempt from temptation.

"Who can say, I have cleansed my heart; I am pure and free from sin?" (Proverbs 20:9).

And if you believe you are not in danger of falling into sin, you are probably more vulnerable than you think.

Seldom do we immediately see our own vulnerabilities. Tim Keller wrote: "Self-deception is not the worst thing you can do, but it's the means by which we do the worst things. The sin that is most distorting your life right now is the one you can't see."

This is why the psalmist prayed, "Keep me from lying to myself; give me the privilege of knowing your instructions" (Psalm 119:29).

READ THE VERSE ON THE OPPOSITE PAGE, THEN REPHRASE AND PERSONALIZE AS A PRAYER FROM YOU TO GOD.

What have you learned from
someone who now walks with a
limp after stepping into sin?

Ponder a time you found yourself
giving into a temptation you
thought you would never embrace.
What surprised you about the
experience? What insights do you
have now about that experience?

Do the failures of others,
especially of those in leadership,
leave you more anxious,
discouraged, or determined not to
follow in their shoes?

MY "AHA"

AWAKEN

WHAT PASSAGE OR INSIGHT FELT MOST PERSONAL FOR YOU?

H EAR

WHAT MIGHT GOD BE SAYING TO YOU?

A SK

WRITE A PRAYER ASKING GOD TO HELP YOU ACKNOWLEDGE YOUR VULNERABILITY TO SIN IN ORDER TO BRING BLESSING INTO YOUR LIFE OR INTO THE LIFE OF SOMEONE YOU KNOW.

> CONFESS YOUR SINS TO
> EACH OTHER AND PRAY
> FOR EACH OTHER SO THAT
> YOU MAY BE HEALED.
> THE EARNEST PRAYER OF
> A RIGHTEOUS PERSON
> HAS GREAT POWER AND
> PRODUCES WONDERFUL
> RESULTS.
>
> (JAMES 5:16)

Reflect on Our Enemy

The reality is that you've got a relentless enemy. He will never give up on bringing you down, so don't assume that you will ever outgrow or age out of any temptation.

By the way, temptation by itself is not sin. Jesus was tempted in every way and yet was without sin. Yes, He was fully divine, but Jesus was also fully human. Our humanity isn't the entire problem; it's our failure to admit our humanity and take the appropriate measures to live within God-designed limits.

Living within limits is the key to godliness. We can be both human and holy. To do so, however, we must do two things:

- Faithfully devote ourselves to making personal application of the Bible.
- Faithfully devote ourselves to living in soul-enriching community.

READ THE VERSE ON THE OPPOSITE PAGE, THEN REPHRASE AND PERSONALIZE AS A PRAYER FROM YOU TO GOD.

If you were to explain to someone how applying Scripture in their daily life and living honestly in community could help them resist giving in to temptation, what would you tell them?

Do you need to come clean about anything? If you were to confess something to someone, who would you choose?

In what ways has our enemy sought to distract, tempt, and destroy you?

MY "AHA"

WAKEN

WHAT PASSAGE OR INSIGHT FELT MOST PERSONAL FOR YOU?

HEAR

WHAT MIGHT GOD BE SAYING TO YOU?

ASK

WRITE A PRAYER ASKING GOD TO HELP YOU BE WISE IN RESISTING OUR ENEMY IN ORDER TO BRING BLESSING INTO YOUR LIFE OR INTO THE LIFE OF SOMEONE YOU KNOW.

"

WHEN A MAN IS GETTING
BETTER, HE UNDERSTANDS
MORE AND MORE CLEARLY
THE EVIL THAT IS STILL
LEFT IN HIM. WHEN A MAN
IS GETTING WORSE, HE
UNDERSTANDS HIS OWN
BADNESS LESS AND LESS.

—C. S. LEWIS

"

REFLECT ON SEXUAL TEMPTATION

Take heart. While sexual enticements are rooted in our humanity and in our society, sexual immorality does not have to be our destiny!

A buddy of mine told me about a Christian leader who confessed, "I wouldn't assume that I'm beyond sexual temptation until I'm in heaven for at least three full days!"

As long as you have a pulse, you'll have some personal battles with temptation.

I want to share three verses with you that can help shed light on the realities (and the bane) of sin:

"If you think you are standing strong, be careful not to fall. The temptations in your life are no different from what others experience. And God is faithful. He will not allow the temptation to be more than you can stand. When you are tempted, he will show you a way out so that you can endure" (1 Corinthians 10:10-13).

"The Spirit who lives in you is greater than the spirit who lives in the world" (I John 4:4).

"For God has not given us a spirit of fear and timidity, but of power, love and self-discipline" (2 Timothy 1:7).

READ THE QUOTE ON THE OPPOSITE PAGE, THEN REPHRASE AND PERSONALIZE AS A PRAYER FROM YOU TO GOD.

How do you reconcile the Bible's position on sexual sin with the world's acceptance of sexual perversion?

What role does fear and timidity play in our vulnerability to sexual sin and sin in general?

Describe a time when you were tempted, and God provided a way out. What path did he provide? Did you take it?

MY "AHA"

Awaken

WHAT PASSAGE OR INSIGHT FELT MOST PERSONAL FOR YOU?

Hear

WHAT MIGHT GOD BE SAYING TO YOU?

Ask

WRITE A PRAYER ASKING GOD TO HELP YOU RECOGNIZE AND RESIST SEXUAL TEMPTATION IN ORDER TO BRING BLESSING INTO YOUR LIFE OR INTO THE LIFE OF SOMEONE YOU KNOW.

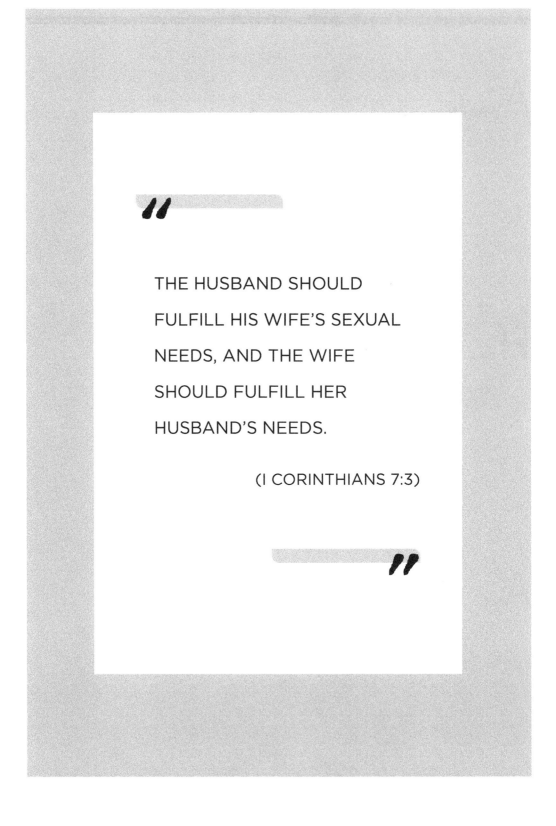

"

THE HUSBAND SHOULD
FULFILL HIS WIFE'S SEXUAL
NEEDS, AND THE WIFE
SHOULD FULFILL HER
HUSBAND'S NEEDS.

(I CORINTHIANS 7:3)

"

REFLECT ON ACCOUNTABILITY

Not one of us is as strong as we wish we were. We all need those who will partner with us in pursuing soul strength. That's why several decades ago, psychologist Dr. John Walker and I began talking weekly and meeting regularly.

Each time we talked, we asked each other five questions that addressed what we were Focusing on, Accepting, Choosing, Enjoying, and Trusting (F.A.C.E.T.). We then customized the questions to reflect what each of us were prioritizing in that season of our lives.

Here are the questions that I invited John to ask me each week:

1. Are you **Focusing** on your wife or fantasizing about someone else?
2. Are you **Accepting** the limitations of others without becoming critical or frustrated?
3. Are you **Choosing** what you want and need to do, or are you obsessing over "should's"?
4. Are you **Enjoying** a sabbath and having fun?
5. Are you **Trusting** that God knows your name? (Isaiah 43:1)

For most of us, asking for accountability almost sounds like inviting someone to snoop around in our dirty laundry.

But accountability isn't about "Thou shalt not...." Accountability is about not walking the journey alone. It's about getting the acceptance and encouragement we need to become our best selves. In fact, these days I rarely seek to hold anyone accountable, rather I simply seek to hold them close.

By God's grace, may we be able to say each day, "I have no secrets, and it's well with my soul."

READ THE VERSE ON THE OPPOSITE PAGE, THEN REPHRASE AND PERSONALIZE AS A PRAYER FROM YOU TO GOD.

What does accountability mean to you? Would you prefer that someone hold you accountable or simply hold you close? What's the difference?

Do you have a confidant with whom you are willing to be 100% known? What do you fear could happen if you did? In what ways might the benefits be worth the risks?

Do you consider the practice of confession to be more of an obligation or a liberation? Describe three benefits of confession that you have personally experienced.

MY "AHA"

Awaken

WHAT PASSAGE OR INSIGHT FELT MOST PERSONAL FOR YOU?

Hear

WHAT MIGHT GOD BE SAYING TO YOU?

Ask

WRITE A PRAYER ASKING GOD TO HELP YOU USE THE POWERFUL RESOURCE OF ACCOUNTBILITY TO BRING BLESSING INTO YOUR LIFE OR INTO THE LIFE OF SOMEONE YOU KNOW.

PURITY OF HEART IS TO WILL
ONE THING.

—SOREN KIERKEGAARD

REFLECT ON THE 4-DS

Inviting others to ask you questions that encourage authenticity and deep conversation is a wonderful tool.

The 4-Ds are a group of questions I crafted years ago. I ask and answer them frequently in Covenant group gatherings, men's groups, and personal interactions:

- What is *delighting* you?
- What is *draining* you?
- What are you *discovering*?
- What are you *determining* to do?

These four questions are gold! They have been powerful for us, for our families, and for all the groups that we lead and facilitate. They work over lunch tables, in small groups, among business leaders, even on the mission field. Twenty pastors serving in the slums of Nairobi are now using them to build healthy relationships with the people they lead.

But someone has to take the lead, both in introducing them and in answering them.

In our soul care covenant group model, these questions are vital. They are part of the rhythm of every gathering and conversation we have, and it has yet to get stale. Just the opposite. This template catalyzes deeper reflection and conversation.

The 4-Ds are life-giving for us and everyone we've been privileged to share them with.

READ THE QUOTE ON THE OPPOSITE PAGE, THEN REPHRASE AND PERSONALIZE AS A PRAYER FROM YOU TO GOD.

How do your daily priorities reflect
your highest values?

How have your personal disciplines
inspired those closest to you?

How have you found questions
such as the 4-Ds helped lead to
deeper conversations?

MY "AHA"

Awaken

What passage or insight felt most personal for you?

Hear

What might God be saying to you?

Ask

Write a prayer asking God to help you make the most of the 4-ds in order to bring blessing into your life or into the life of someone you know.

SABBATH REFLECTION

Soul work is slow work

WHAT IS *DELIGHTING* YOU?

WHAT IS *DRAINING* YOU?

WHAT ARE YOU *DISCOVERING*?

WHAT ARE YOU *DETERMINING TO DO*?

WERE ANY OF YOUR ANSWERS INFLUENCED BY YOUR RECENT READINGS? IF SO, HOW?

7

LIVE GENEROUSLY

Read Chapter 7 from the companion book, Soul Strength: Rhythms for Thriving.

When our son encouraged us to host an exchange student, I didn't want to add anything more to our lives. Then he challenged me by saying, "Well, Dad, you know what you always say about embracing ministry opportunities!"

The next thing I knew, we had another sixteen-year-old living with us for a year.

The following summer, Olli's family came to vacation with us from Germany before taking him home. When Linda and I met Olli's introverted sister—the one Olli said would never be brave enough to spend a year away from home—I teased, "So Steffi, are you coming to live with us next year?"

When she said yes, everyone was surprised—especially me!

While I never intended to open our home and our lives like this, I thank God that I did. Olli later married our youngest daughter's best friend. Steffi married a German pastor, and they spent their honeymoon with us! Our lives are intertwined, and we will be forever grateful.

After our gift of hospitality to them, we received a stunning surprise of generosity in return. Olli and Steffi's parents hosted our entire family for a memorable tour of their country. Their generosity amazed us!

Jesus said, "Give, and you will receive. Your gift will return to you in full – pressed down, shaken together to make room for more, running over, and poured into your lap. The amount you give will determine the amount you get back" (Luke 6:38).

ENJOY THE FOLLOWING REFLECTIONS:

- ☐ Reflect on Enough
- ☐ Reflect on Faithfulness
- ☐ Reflect on Joy
- ☐ Reflect on Generosity
- ☐ Reflect on Legacy
- ☐ Sabbath Reflection

YOU WILL BE MADE RICH
IN EVERY WAY SO THAT
YOU CAN BE GENEROUS
ON EVERY OCCASION,
AND THROUGH US YOUR
GENEROSITY WILL RESULT
IN THANKSGIVING TO GOD.

(2 CORINTHIANS 9:11 NIV)

REFLECT ON ENOUGH

Have you yet responded to the bold advice to trust God and tithe? The reality is that at some point we all managed to survive on at least 10% less than we do now. In truth many of us are far richer than we ever expected to be.

The average home is not only three times larger than the homes when I was growing up, but are now filled with literally thousands of little luxuries that go unnoticed. That's true for most all of us even though we know that the most important things in life aren't things at all.

C. S. Lewis wrote in *Mere Christianity*, "I do not believe one can settle how much we ought to give. I am afraid the only safe rule is to give more than we can spare. In other words, if our expenditure on comforts, luxuries, amusements, etc., is up to the standard common among those with the same income as our own, we are probably giving away too little."

READ THE VERSE ON THE OPPOSITE PAGE, THEN REPHRASE AND PERSONALIZE AS A PRAYER FROM YOU TO GOD.

What does having enough mean to you? Do you have enough today?

Describe a time you felt a nudge in your spirit to be generous with someone. How did you respond? Did you ever regret your response?

Describe an experience when you were surprised and blessed by someone's generosity towards you.

MY "AHA"

Awaken

WHAT PASSAGE OR INSIGHT FELT MOST PERSONAL FOR YOU?

Hear

WHAT MIGHT GOD BE SAYING TO YOU?

Ask

WRITE A PRAYER ASKING GOD TO HELP YOU PRACTICE CONTENTMENT AND GENEROSITY TO BRING BLESSING INTO YOUR LIFE OR INTO THE LIFE OF SOMEONE YOU KNOW.

"

BRING THE WHOLE TITHE
INTO THE STOREHOUSE,
THAT THERE MAY BE FOOD
IN MY HOUSE. 'TEST ME
IN THIS,' SAYS THE LORD
ALMIGHTY, 'AND SEE IF I
WILL NOT THROW OPEN THE
FLOODGATES OF HEAVEN.'

(MALACHI 3:10 NIV)

"

Reflect on Faithfulness

We are never more like God than when we give. Jesus made that clear in one of the most famous accounts of his ministry recorded in Luke 21:1-3 (NIV):

"As Jesus looked up, he saw the rich putting their gifts into the temple treasury. He also saw a poor widow put in two very small copper coins. 'Truly I tell you,' he said, 'this poor widow has put in more than all the others. All these people gave their gifts out of their wealth; but she out of her poverty put in all she had to live on.'"

Pastor Gregg Surratt has made the statement that Jesus is taking notes on our generosity.

My parents faithfully modeled tithing and generosity for me. One of my early memories was putting a dime of every dollar I earned in my offering envelope every Sunday. I remember sitting in church anticipating the offering and thinking: *Whoever opens this envelope may think my dime is no big deal. But it's my tithe of my dollar. I want to do this because I want to be faithful to God and to His church!*

When our kids were growing up our budget was tight so we taught them the 10/10/80 plan. That's give at least ten percent. Save at least 10 percent and carefully manage the rest. That pattern has served our family and church family very well over the years.

READ THE VERSE ON THE OPPOSITE PAGE, THEN REPHRASE AND PERSONALIZE AS A PRAYER FROM YOU TO GOD.

What are some of your experiences
with tithing? Is it something your
parents embraced? Is it something
you do today? Is it a new idea for
you?

If you tithed and even gave a
little past your comfort zone on a
regular basis, what would happen?
What impact might that have on
your life? Your relationships? Your
perspective?

What is the biggest obstacle you
face when it comes to tithing and/
or giving beyond? Brainstorm three
solutions to that obstacle. Are you
willing to give one of them a try?

MY "AHA"

A_{WAKEN}

W_{HAT PASSAGE OR INSIGHT FELT MOST PERSONAL FOR YOU?}

H_{EAR}

W_{HAT MIGHT} G_{OD BE SAYING TO YOU?}

A_{SK}

W_{RITE A PRAYER ASKING} G_{OD TO HELP YOU EMBRACE THE DISCIPLINE OF FAITHFUL GIVING TO BRING BLESSING INTO YOUR LIFE OR INTO THE LIFE OF SOMEONE YOU KNOW.}

"

FOR GOD LOVES A PERSON
WHO GIVES CHEERFULLY.
AND GOD WILL GENEROUSLY
PROVIDE ALL YOU WANT AND
NEED. THEN YOU WILL HAVE
EVERYTHING YOU NEED AND
PLENTY LEFT OVER TO SHARE
WITH OTHERS.

(2 CORINTHIANS 9:7-8)

"

REFLECT ON JOY

Studies show that many people report their happiness is linked to simplicity and generosity. In fact, it's been documented that self-esteem goes up as giving goes up!

Joy is the goal. In fact, whenever Linda and I have dipped our toes in the deepest waters of generous giving, we have also experienced the deepest joy.

Money in the hands of a generous person is a force multiplier. It's both a test and a trust. What we do with it becomes a testimony. Making money to make a difference is a noble thing. Lavish giving is God's standard for His people, not lavish living.

As a single mother in our congregation once told me: *"I love tithing because it makes me feel so rich!"*

READ THE VERSE ON THE OPPOSITE PAGE, THEN REPHRASE AND PERSONALIZE AS A PRAYER FROM YOU TO GOD.

To what degree do you see yourself
as blessed to be a blessing?
Describe ways that you've been
blessed by blessing others.

Have you ever longed for a simpler
life as a means of experiencing
less stress and more joy? What
is keeping you from embracing a
simpler lifestyle?

When you hear about people who
have increased their giving to God
and others to 20, 30, even 50
percent of their income, what are
your thoughts? Do you think them
foolish? Do you wish you could do
the same?

MY "AHA"

A**WAKEN**

WHAT PASSAGE OR INSIGHT FELT MOST PERSONAL FOR YOU?

H**EAR**

WHAT MIGHT GOD BE SAYING TO YOU?

A**SK**

WRITE A PRAYER ASKING GOD TO HELP YOU EXPERIENCE THE JOY OF GIVING IN ORDER TO BRING BLESSING INTO YOUR LIFE OR INTO THE LIFE OF SOMEONE YOU KNOW.

"

LIGHT SHINES IN THE
DARKNESS FOR THE GODLY.
THEY ARE GENEROUS,
COMPASSIONATE, AND
RIGHTEOUS. GOOD COMES
TO THOSE WHO LEND MONEY
GENEROUSLY AND CONDUCT
THEIR BUSINESS FAIRLY.

(PSALM 112:1, 4-5)

"

REFLECT ON GENEROSITY

Even though God's Word is clear on the topic of money, most of God's people ignore it. Far less than ten percent of Christians even give the base biblical amount of ten percent.

Tithing is the beginning of our stewardship, not the ending. Randy Alcorn has said, "God prospers me not to raise my standard of living but to raise my standard of giving."

As I see it, there are three levels of giving:

The Devotion Level: Faithfulness in returning the first ten percent. A tithe is a great place to start but a lousy place to stop!

The Inspiration Level: Generosity prompted by special needs or opportunities. We all need to be open to the prompt to share.

The Revelation Level: Responding to a clear call of God with radical, even life-altering generosity. Something far beyond the "reasonable."

READ THE VERSE ON THE OPPOSITE PAGE, THEN REPHRASE AND PERSONALIZE AS A PRAYER FROM YOU TO GOD.

Review the three levels of giving.
Which level most resonates for you
right now and why?

What is keeping you from
increasing your giving to God and
others?

Why do you think the topic
of tithing and generosity is
uncomfortable for many believers?
Is it uncomfortable for you?

MY "AHA"

Awaken

WHAT PASSAGE OR INSIGHT FELT MOST PERSONAL FOR YOU?

Hear

WHAT MIGHT GOD BE SAYING TO YOU?

Ask

WRITE A PRAYER ASKING GOD TO HELP YOU FALL IN LOVE WITH RADICAL GENEROSITY TO BRING BLESSING INTO YOUR LIFE OR INTO THE LIFE OF SOMEONE YOU KNOW.

"

THOSE WHO ARE RIGHTEOUS WILL BE LONG REMEMBERED. ... THEIR GOOD DEEDS WILL BE REMEMBERED FOREVER. THEY WILL HAVE INFLUENCE AND HONOR.

(PSALM 112:6-9)

"

Reflect on Legacy

In my Bible I penciled this, *"Joyful generosity is the finest legacy."*

I once enjoyed a memorable conversation on an airplane. I had just met the man seated near me the night before at a leadership meeting. We were both surprised to discover we were traveling on the same flight and seated in the same row with an open seat between us.

I rarely talk on planes, much less have an actual conversation. This is one I'll never forget.

As the flight progressed so did our personal connection as we began to talk about the things that mattered most to each of us. That's when Jack made a statement unlike any I had ever heard from anyone else before.

"Alan," he said, "I just want to be remembered as a generous man!"

How do you want to be remembered? On the last day it won't matter what sort of house we lived in or car we drove or the size of our retirement account. The only thing that will matter is what we did *with* Jesus and what we did *for* Jesus.

Rather than living with a scarcity mentality, we ought to live with a generosity mentality. God blesses us so we can be a blessing to others—with our money, but also with our time and talents.

Read the verse on the opposite page, then rephrase and personalize as a prayer from you to God.

How do you want to be
remembered?

What pattern of generosity do
you hope to instill in your own
children?

What does a "scarcity mindset"
mean to you? Do you have one?
How is a scarcity mindset linked
to misplaced trust?

MY "AHA"

Awaken

WHAT PASSAGE OR INSIGHT FELT MOST PERSONAL FOR YOU?

Hear

WHAT MIGHT GOD BE SAYING TO YOU?

Ask

WRITE A PRAYER ASKING GOD TO GUIDE YOU AS YOU CONSIDER YOUR LEGACY, AND IN DOING SO BRING BLESSING INTO YOUR LIFE OR INTO THE LIFE OF SOMEONE YOU KNOW.

SABBATH REFLECTION

Soul work is slow work

WHAT IS *DELIGHTING* YOU?

WHAT IS *DRAINING* YOU?

WHAT ARE YOU *DISCOVERING*?

WHAT ARE YOU *DETERMINING* TO DO?

WERE ANY OF YOUR ANSWERS INFLUENCED BY YOUR RECENT READINGS? IF SO, HOW?

8

ACCEPT YOUR LIMITS

Read Chapter 8 from the companion book, Soul Strength: Rhythms for Thriving.

Limits can be frustrating. I know because I'm living with some frustrating limits right now in my eyesight, balance, and physical strength.

While I can't run without knee pain, I can still hike or bike for hours if I stay hydrated and pay attention. I still enjoy high energy and daily outdoor activities. In other words, I'm refusing to "let the old man in" by lounging in a recliner watching hours of TV and eating big bags of Doritos.

Wherever we experience limits—in our bodies, health, finances, careers—it reminds us that there are simply some things in life that are out of our control.

But not everything, which is why I frequently return to the prayer of Reinhold Niebuhr. You're familiar with the first part but probably not the rest:

God, give me the serenity to accept the things I cannot change, courage to change the things I can, and wisdom to know the difference.

Living one day at a time; enjoying one moment at a time;
accepting hardship as a pathway to peace; taking, as Jesus did, this sinful world
as it is, not as I would have it; trusting that You will make all things right if I
surrender to Your will; that I may be reasonably happy in this life,
And supremely happy with You forever in the next. Amen.

ENJOY THE FOLLOWING REFLECTIONS:

- ☐ Reflect on Boundaries
- ☐ Reflect on Sabbath
- ☐ Reflect on Pondering
- ☐ Reflect on Cheerfulness
- ☐ Reflect on Good Advice
- ☐ Sabbath Reflection

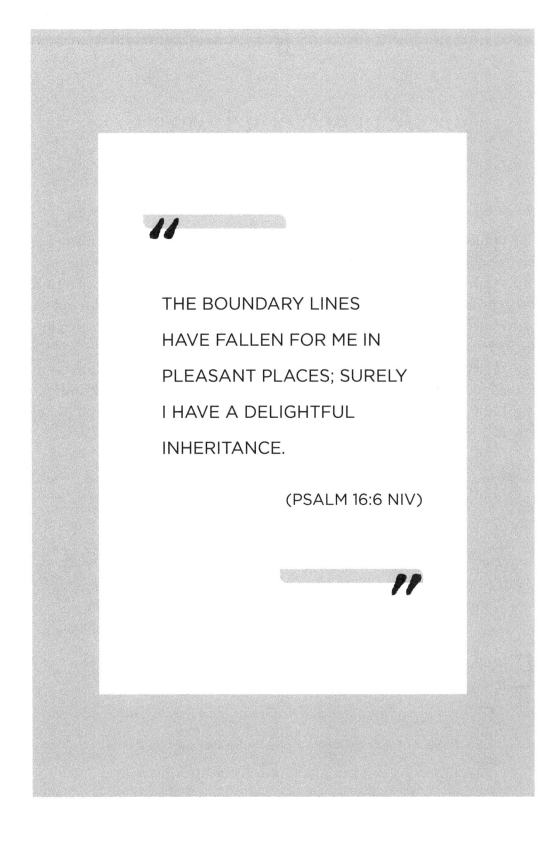

THE BOUNDARY LINES
HAVE FALLEN FOR ME IN
PLEASANT PLACES; SURELY
I HAVE A DELIGHTFUL
INHERITANCE.

(PSALM 16:6 NIV)

REFLECT ON BOUNDARIES

Several years ago, I helped a friend of mine, Boulder County Sheriff Joe Pelle, put on a seminar for the cops in our region. The seminar featured Kevin Gilmartin, author of *Emotional Survival for Law Enforcement.* That's where I learned about the emotional toll of hyper-vigilance.

People who are always on full alert at work facing challenges and threats can crash when they are off duty. Why? Because we're designed to handle just so much stress and adrenaline before there's a price to pay.

In fact, too much of pretty much anything—work, food, social media—takes a toll.

Healthy limits and boundaries are among God's gifts to us all.

To thrive, we need others in our lives who understand the power of boundaries and help us do the same

You don't need a lot of people to do that. You just need the right people—people who have the credibility to remind us to acknowledge our limits. Boundaries are good for your soul.

READ THE VERSE ON THE OPPOSITE PAGE, THEN REPHRASE AND PERSONALIZE AS A PRAYER FROM YOU TO GOD.

What feels like too much in your
life right now? What healthy
boundaries or limits are being
exceeded?

Describe a situation when you
respected a healthy limit or
boundary that was set for you,
or you set and kept a healthy
boundary for yourself.

What do you find frustrating or
disappointing when it comes
to boundaries? Setting them?
Keeping them? Asking others to
respect yours?

MY "AHA"

WAKEN

WHAT PASSAGE OR INSIGHT FELT MOST PERSONAL FOR YOU?

HEAR

WHAT MIGHT GOD BE SAYING TO YOU?

ASK

WRITE A PRAYER ASKING GOD TO HELP YOU EMBRACE HEALTHY BOUNDARIES TO BRING BLESSING INTO YOUR LIFE OR INTO THE LIFE OF SOMEONE YOU KNOW.

"

THOSE WHO ARE WISE WILL
TAKE THIS TO HEART. THEY
WILL SEE IN OUR HISTORY
THE FAITHFUL LOVE OF THE
LORD.

(PSALM 107:43)

"

REFLECT ON SABBATH

When it comes to exceeding life's speed limits, I'm not alone. This is why the Lord instituted the Sabbath rhythm. The word literally means to stop!

God's people were told not just to take a break, but to set aside one day a week for worship, rest, and renewal of the soul. Sabbath is intended to be a life-enriching gift of God to us all. In the revised edition of her classic book, *Soul Feast,* Marjorie Thompson includes a chapter on "Reclaiming Sabbath Time: Reclaiming the Sacred Art of Ceasing."

She says: "Valuing and guarding the sacred rhythm of sabbath is a radical choice, particularly in a culture as devoted as ours to production and achievement."

She began the chapter recalling when a friend referred to *"the beauty of the borders."* Flora Wuellner reminded everyone that landscapes are made more beautiful by fences, hedges and flowerbeds. It's certainly true in our yard. Several years ago, we added tons of rock, mulch, and fresh edging to better define the landscape. As a result, there's hardly a day that goes by that I don't enjoy a visual feast.

There's definite value in clear definition of our landscape and our lives.

READ THE VERSE ON THE OPPOSITE PAGE, THEN REPHRASE AND PERSONALIZE AS A PRAYER FROM YOU TO GOD.

When do you stop and enjoy rest and renewal? How often? What does that look like in your life?

If you don't currently set aside a whole day each week for rest and renewal, how might your life be different if you did? Identify pros and cons.

Identify five or six things that would make a day set apart feel worshipful, restful, and renewing?

MY "AHA"

Awaken

WHAT PASSAGE OR INSIGHT FELT MOST PERSONAL FOR YOU?

Hear

WHAT MIGHT GOD BE SAYING TO YOU?

Ask

WRITE A PRAYER ASKING GOD TO HELP YOU GUARD THE SACRED RHYTHM OF SABBATH REST TO BRING BLESSING INTO YOUR LIFE OR INTO THE LIFE OF SOMEONE YOU KNOW.

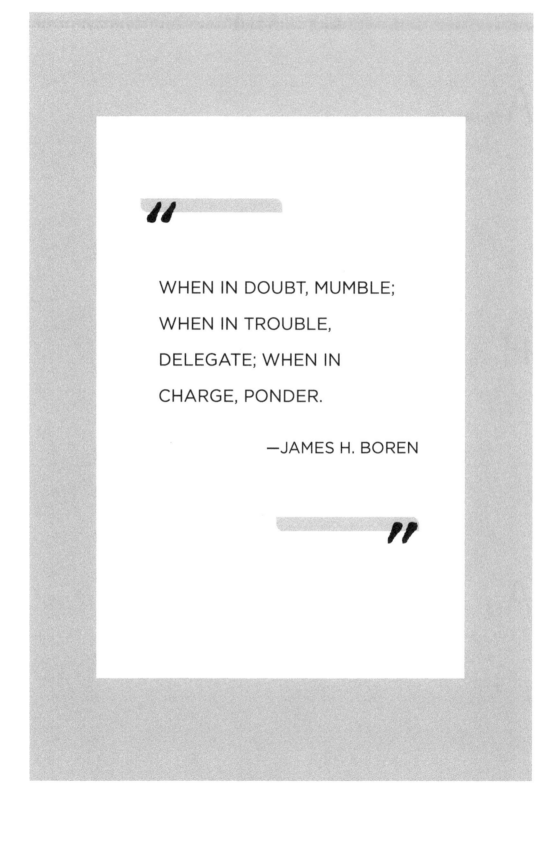

WHEN IN DOUBT, MUMBLE;
WHEN IN TROUBLE,
DELEGATE; WHEN IN
CHARGE, PONDER.

—JAMES H. BOREN

REFLECT ON PONDERING

Our leadership culture is long on performance metrics but short on pondering. This I know: my reflectiveness is key to my effectiveness. The more time I invest in reflection, the more effective my life investments seem to be. This is part of my daily, weekly, monthly, and annual soul-enriching rhythm.

There is great value in pondering. Sometimes I follow a structure called RAP, which means Review-Analyze-Plan. I find that it consistently leads to soul-gratifying discovery.

- Review: "I pondered the direction of my life, and I turned to follow your laws" (Psalm 119:59).
- Analyze: "Speak, Lord, your servant is listening" (I Samuel 3:9).
- Plan: "If you plan to do good, you will receive unfailing love and faithfulness" (Proverbs 14:22).

I use a simple bullet outline to take note of the highlights in each category. Then I write a few paragraphs of analysis. Finally, I use a few more bullets to identify upcoming opportunities I'm intending to pursue.

READ THE QUOTE ON THE OPPOSITE PAGE, THEN REPHRASE AND PERSONALIZE AS A PRAYER FROM YOU TO GOD.

What does the idea of pondering mean to you?

Identify six ways that more reflection could improve effectiveness in at least one area of your life.

How have changes in our society and lifestyles in the past fifty years helped or hindered our opportunity or ability for reflection?

MY "AHA"

Awaken

What passage or insight felt most personal for you?

Hear

What might God be saying to you?

Ask

Write a prayer asking God to help you experience the power of pondering to bring blessing into your life or into the life of someone you know.

"

FOR THE HAPPY HEART, LIFE
IS A CONTINUAL FEAST.

(PROVERBS 15:15)

LET ALL THAT I AM PRAISE
THE LORD; WITH MY WHOLE
HEART, I WILL PRAISE HIS
HOLY NAME. LET ALL THAT I
AM PRAISE THE LORD; MAY
I NEVER FORGET THE GOOD
THINGS HE DOES FOR ME.

(PSALM 103:1-2)

"

REFLECT ON CHEERFULNESS

These are hard times. But whenever I overdose on despairing media messages, God's Word helps me to reframe everything. Life is a non-stop litany of hard hits and heart hits, but Jesus said: "Take heart! I have overcome the world" (John 16:33 NIV).

Now when I quickly review the local, national, and world news I already know it's going to be bad news. That's why I try to approach the news with a determined cheerfulness. First, I seek to severely limit my exposure to the bad news of the day. Then when I do briefly read or review it, I do so against the banner of my Lord's call to take heart—He has overcome the world!

What have you been saying to yourself lately? Dr. David Martyn Lloyd-Jones, a physician turned pastor, said: "The central cause of spiritual depression is due to the fact that you are listening to yourself instead of talking to yourself!"

I for one need to talk to myself every day, all day. The message I repeatedly need to hear is clear:

- "Cheer up! There is One who redeems all things!"
- "Cheer up! The position of Savior has been taken!"
- "Cheer up! Now is not forever!"
- "Cheer up! The purpose of the Lord will prevail!"
- "Cheer up! By God's grace the best is yet to be!"
- "Cheer up! Jesus has overcome the world!"

Read the verses on the opposite page, then rephrase and personalize as a prayer from you to God.

Have you heard the phrase
"attitude determines altitude"?
What do those words mean to you?

When you are feeling anything but
cheerful and want to elevate your
mood or adjust your attitude, what
thoughts or actions have helped
you in the past?

Is cheerfulness more of an
emotion or perspective? Defend
your answer.

MY "AHA"

Awaken

WHAT PASSAGE OR INSIGHT FELT MOST PERSONAL FOR YOU?

-

Hear

WHAT MIGHT GOD BE SAYING TO YOU?

Ask

WRITE A PRAYER ASKING GOD TO HELP YOU CHOOSE CHEERFULNESS TO BRING BLESSING INTO YOUR LIFE OR INTO THE LIFE OF SOMEONE YOU KNOW.

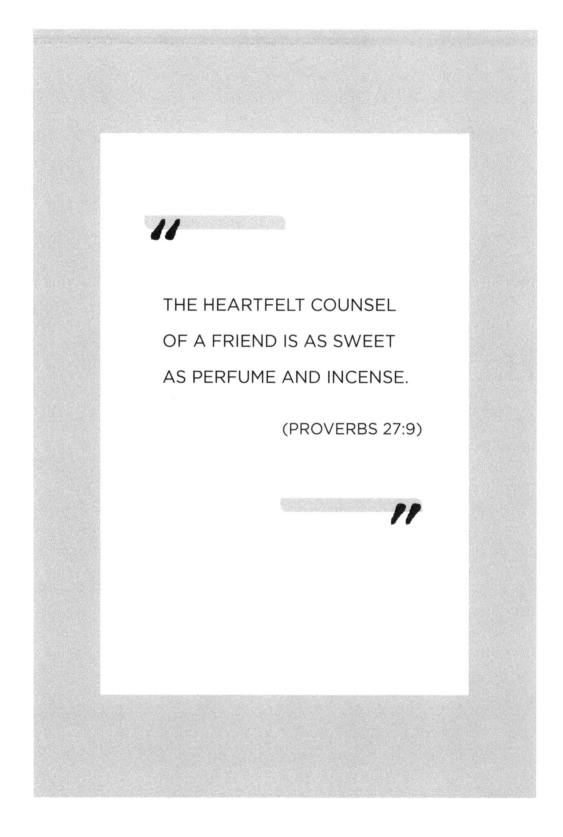

THE HEARTFELT COUNSEL

OF A FRIEND IS AS SWEET

AS PERFUME AND INCENSE.

(PROVERBS 27:9)

REFLECT ON GOOD ADVICE

Who knows you well enough to speak the truth in love to you?

My closest friends take turns speaking the truth in love to me. Often, their words are deeply encouraging. I will always treasure the words of Cam Huxford when I was reeling from overlapping crises. I was so emotionally exhausted that I wasn't appreciative of God's sustaining grace.

That's when Cam said to me, "You encountered the perfect storm but still got the ship safely back to port." He added, "In Savannah we say, 'you can prepare for a storm but you can't prepare for a hurricane—you can only pray to survive!'"

I later found these verses in Psalm 107:29-32:

> He calmed the storm to a whisper
> > and stilled the waves.
> What a blessing was that stillness
> > as he brought them safely into harbor!
> Let them praise the Lord for his great love
> > and for the wonderful things he has done for them.
> Let them exalt him publicly before the congregation
> > and before the leaders of the nation.

Crises are inevitable in leadership and life. Everyone needs a safe person to help process the hits and hurts we all experience.

READ THE VERSE ON THE OPPOSITE PAGE, THEN REPHRASE AND PERSONALIZE AS A PRAYER FROM YOU TO GOD.

Who among your friends are wise
advice-givers? When was the last
time you solicited or followed their
counsel?

On a scale of one to ten (ten being
great) how are you at seeking and
following good advice? How has
this helped or hindered you?

What challenges or decisions are
you facing today that good counsel
could assist you with?

MY "AHA"

Awaken

What passage or insight felt most personal for you?

Hear

What might God be saying to you?

Ask

Write a prayer asking God to help you seek and recognize good advice to bring blessing into your life or into the life of someone you know.

SABBATH REFLECTION

Soul work is slow work

WHAT IS *DELIGHTING* YOU?

WHAT IS *DRAINING* YOU?

WHAT ARE YOU *DISCOVERING*?

WHAT ARE YOU *DETERMINING* TO DO?

WERE ANY OF YOUR ANSWERS INFLUENCED BY YOUR RECENT READINGS? IF SO, HOW?

9

PURSUE THE BIGGER YES

Read Chapter 9 from the companion book, Soul Strength: Rhythms for Thriving.

Gonzalo was in a dark place when the light finally came on. After years as a gang leader, he was finally convicted of violent crimes and sent to Federal prison. It was there that the full realization of his sin and shame engulfed him. He felt hopeless. In desperation he cried out to God.

God's answer was stunning: "My children, my children, take care of my children!"

Gonzalo was not a believer or even a churchgoing guy. Still, he immediately knew he was to turn his life over to God and serve Him for the rest of his life. After he prayed in his prison cell, God miraculously changed his heart.

Gonzalo has shared his heart-changing story with our covenant group. We've seen the results as he reflects uncommon kindness to all.

"The bigger yes" that God gave to Gonzalo turned him from leading bad guys in doing bad stuff to leading God's people in doing good stuff! He is now embracing a higher calling and serving as an outreach pastor in Florida.

A high calling changes everything!

Are you ready to say "Yes!"?

ENJOY THE FOLLOWING REFLECTIONS:

- ☐ Reflect on The Bigger Yes
- ☐ Reflect on Calling
- ☐ Reflect on Certainty
- ☐ Reflect on Hardship
- ☐ Reflect on Significance
- ☐ Sabbath Reflection

"

TRUST IN THE LORD WITH
ALL YOUR HEART AND
LEAN NOT ON YOUR OWN
UNDERSTANDING; IN ALL
YOUR WAYS SUBMIT TO HIM,
AND HE WILL MAKE YOUR
PATHS STRAIGHT.

(PROVERBS 3:5-6 NIV)

"

Reflect on The Bigger Yes

Someone once said that to leave a lasting legacy we must live for something definite.

Over the years I've called it the Bigger Yes!

I believe there is no substitute for having an unshakable sense that there is something big in your life that must be pursued and addressed right away!

Friends are always part of the Bigger Yes of my life.

It's been said that you can't go out and make old friends, you either have them or you don't! I'm blessed to have many good friends, both old and new. Virtually all of them have been made the same way . . . slowly. I have cultivated them over the years by making time for them as they have made time for me.

Are friends a part of your Bigger Yes in life?

I hope so. Because if you don't make time for your friends, you won't have any.

Read the verse on the opposite page, then rephrase and personalize as a prayer from you to God.

Name several things you pursue
intentionally and with a sense of
purpose.

Are deep friendships on that list?
If not, why not? And if they are,
what do you do to intentionally say
yes to these kinds of friendships?
Could you do more?

How big a challenge is loneliness
in your life, and how do you
manage that?

MY "AHA"

AWAKEN

WHAT PASSAGE OR INSIGHT FELT MOST PERSONAL FOR YOU?

HEAR

WHAT MIGHT GOD BE SAYING TO YOU?

ASK

WRITE A PRAYER ASKING GOD TO HELP YOU REFLECT ON THE BIGGER YES TO BRING BLESSING INTO YOUR LIFE OR INTO THE LIFE OF SOMEONE YOU KNOW.

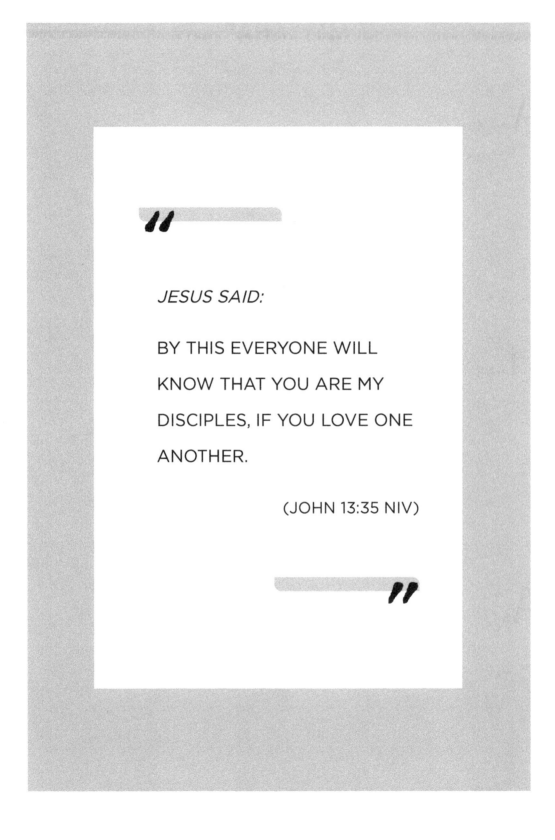

JESUS SAID:

BY THIS EVERYONE WILL
KNOW THAT YOU ARE MY
DISCIPLES, IF YOU LOVE ONE
ANOTHER.

(JOHN 13:35 NIV)

REFLECT ON CALLING

What is your Bigger Yes? Do your closest friends know what it is?

The Apostle Paul wrote to Timothy, "But you, Timothy, certainly know what I teach, and how I live, and what my purpose in life is. You know my faith, patience, love, and endurance" (2 Timothy 3:10).

We all need to see ourselves—and to be seen by those who know us best—as devoted to something that is bigger than ourselves.

The things to which we feel called--our divine assignments—keep us energized and give us a reason to lean into the future.

It's been said that your vision is whatever you'd delay going to heaven in order to accomplish. That's the ultimate *Big Yes!* In I Timothy 1:1 the Message version puts it this way: "I, Paul, am an apostle on special assignment for Christ, our living hope."

Read the verse on the opposite page, then rephrase and personalize as a prayer from you to God.

Do you have a sense that you are on a special assignment? Are you on a mission that matters? If your answer is yes, describe what it is. If your answer is no, how would life feel different if you were?

Accomplishing something big is great—but it is the journey there that provides the spark to our days and the opportunity for growth. What makes a calling and mission rewarding?

Do you feel that some callings are greater than others, or just different?

MY "AHA"

AWAKEN

WHAT PASSAGE OR INSIGHT FELT MOST PERSONAL FOR YOU?

HEAR

WHAT MIGHT GOD BE SAYING TO YOU?

ASK

WRITE A PRAYER ASKING GOD TO HELP YOU EMBRACE YOUR DIVINE ASSIGNMENT TO BRING BLESSING INTO YOUR LIFE OR INTO THE LIFE OF SOMEONE YOU KNOW.

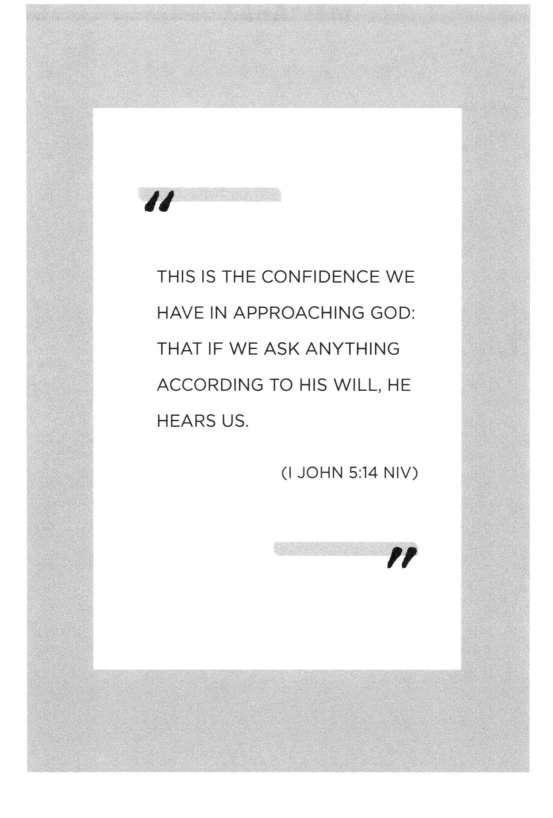

THIS IS THE CONFIDENCE WE
HAVE IN APPROACHING GOD:
THAT IF WE ASK ANYTHING
ACCORDING TO HIS WILL, HE
HEARS US.

(I JOHN 5:14 NIV)

REFLECT ON CERTAINTY

At times everyone wrestles with a lack of clarity and confidence. We all wrestle with doubts about tomorrow or the day after, doubts about next month or next year. No one can ever fully know what the future holds. Only God knows the future and He's not telling. "The LORD our God has secrets known to no one. We are not accountable for them…" (Deuteronomy 29:29).

If we're waiting until we have a full understanding of every ramification of every commitment, we will never commit to anything. For example, the very reason that marriage vows are made is that commitment is necessary for the fulfillment of them. The same is true in our relationship with Christ.

Until we make a heartfelt commitment to follow Him we will be immobilized. Until there is commitment there is always hesitancy. Yet, when there is commitment there is increasing certainty—not certainty about everything, just about the next thing.

READ THE VERSE ON THE OPPOSITE PAGE, THEN REPHRASE AND PERSONALIZE AS A PRAYER FROM YOU TO GOD.

What are your thoughts about
the tension between certainty,
confidence, and faith?

When you can't see the entire
path before you, how comfortable
are you moving forward? Is it
enough to be able to see your next
step without seeing beyond that?
What holds you back?

How do you discern between
"stepping out in faith" and being
foolish, reckless, or uninformed?

MY "AHA"

Awaken

WHAT PASSAGE OR INSIGHT FELT MOST PERSONAL FOR YOU?

Hear

WHAT MIGHT GOD BE SAYING TO YOU?

Ask

WRITE A PRAYER ASKING GOD TO HELP YOU EMBRACE THE BEAUTY OF COMMITMENT TO BRING BLESSING INTO YOUR LIFE OR INTO THE LIFE OF SOMEONE YOU KNOW.

"

THEN JESUS SAID TO HIS
DISCIPLES, 'WHOEVER
WANTS TO BE MY DISCIPLE
MUST DENY THEMSELVES
AND TAKE UP THEIR CROSS
AND FOLLOW ME.'

(MATTHEW 6:24 NIV)

"

REFLECT ON HARDSHIP

Scripture makes it clear that "we must suffer many hardships to enter the Kingdom of God" (Acts 14:22)—and that "everyone who wants to live a godly life in Christ Jesus will suffer" (2 Timothy 3:12).

Hardships, illness, and suffering may involve tears, misunderstandings, betrayal, abandonment, heartache, and hard financial times. For some, it means martyrdom.

It's been said that a season of suffering is worth enduring for a clearer vision of God. We don't get to choose our callings and assignments, but we do get to choose our attitude in them and toward them. We certainly don't get to select the sufferings that will accompany them.

But whatever we suffer because of our commitment to Christ, we suffer on purpose for Christ. That's what makes the calling of the disciple so demanding and yet so fulfilling.

PERSONALIZE AND REPHRASE THE VERSE ON THE OPPOSITE PAGE AS A PRAYER FROM YOU TO GOD.

What is the hardest thing God has
called you to do? Do you feel that
you suffered in the process?

What are some ways we can
keep hardships from making us
question our calling?

What are your thoughts about the
role of a supportive community in
helping us navigate the hardships
that come with a difficult
assignment?

MY "AHA"

AWAKEN

WHAT PASSAGE OR INSIGHT FELT MOST PERSONAL FOR YOU?

HEAR

WHAT MIGHT GOD BE SAYING TO YOU?

ASK

WRITE A PRAYER ASKING GOD TO HELP YOU SEE HIM CLEARLY, DESPITE HARDSHIP, TO BRING BLESSING INTO YOUR LIFE OR INTO THE LIFE OF SOMEONE YOU KNOW.

"

JOY COMES FROM

SEEING THE COMPLETE

FULFILLMENT OF THE

SPECIFIC PURPOSE FOR

WHICH I WAS CREATED AND

BORN AGAIN, NOT FROM

SUCCESSFULLY DOING

SOMETHING OF MY OWN

CHOOSING.

—OSWALD CHAMBERS

"

REFLECT ON SIGNIFICANCE

These days we have made an idol out of being significant in the eyes of the world rather than humbly serving the One who is significant. Too many times we are only willing to step up and serve if we get to pick the inspiring assignment! What if our next assignment doesn't turn out to be a really big one?

Could it be that the next assignment for each of us will be a small one, at least in the eyes of the world?

No one makes one single, big commitment that lasts a lifetime without a series of small daily re-commitments along the way. The daily commitments of your life define your life. You see, God's blessing doesn't merely rest upon those who make a commitment, but upon those who keep a commitment! This may not be something that ever appears on our resume, but it may become a lasting part of our legacy.

As Oswald Chambers noted: "Drudgery is the touchstone of character. The great hindrance in spiritual life is that we will look for big things to do. 'Jesus took a towel… and began to wash the disciples' feet.'"

READ THE QUOTE ON THE OPPOSITE PAGE, THEN REPHRASE AND PERSONALIZE AS A PRAYER FROM YOU TO GOD.

What makes you feel significant?

What are your thoughts on mundane tasks or assignments? Do you resent them? Embrace them? Do you believe they are all you are worthy of tackling?

How closely is your sense of significance tied to the scale of your accomplishments?

MY "AHA"

A_{WAKEN}

WHAT PASSAGE OR INSIGHT FELT MOST PERSONAL FOR YOU?

H_{EAR}

WHAT MIGHT GOD BE SAYING TO YOU?

A_{SK}

WRITE A PRAYER ASKING GOD TO HELP YOU FIND YOUR SIGNIFICANCE IN HIM IN ORDER TO BRING BLESSING INTO YOUR LIFE OR INTO THE LIFE OF SOMEONE YOU KNOW.

SABBATH REFLECTION

Soul work is slow work

WHAT IS *DELIGHTING* YOU?

WHAT IS *DRAINING* YOU?

WHAT ARE YOU *DISCOVERING*?

WHAT ARE YOU *DETERMINING* TO DO?

WERE ANY OF YOUR ANSWERS INFLUENCED BY YOUR RECENT READINGS? IF SO, HOW?

10

LIVE GRATEFULLY

Read Chapter 10 from the companion book, Soul Strength: Rhythms for Thriving.

Betsy had been hospitalized for a week when doctors, unable to identify the cause of her symptoms, transferred her to a larger hospital. She was deeply discouraged the day she arrived there by ambulance.

Betsy's new nurse, a young woman from Kenya, introduced herself as Olive. She explained she'd chosen this as her American name because she felt her African name was too difficult for Americans to pronounce.

Realizing how discouraged Betsy was, Olive said something surprising. "You know, there are many people in my country who would happily trade places with you!"

That stunning statement instantly shifted Betsy's perspective. She immediately started seeing the blessings that surrounded her even in the hospital: A loving husband. A gifted medical staff. A private room, a clean bathroom, even hot water!

Betsy's attitude of intentional, determined gratitude accompanied the healing process that continues to this day.

Betsy says Olive was a gift from God and an agent of peace. Betsy later reflected that just as an olive branch is a symbol of peace, Olive provided Betsy with a clear sign that God was with her.

ENJOY THE FOLLOWING REFLECTIONS:

- ☐ Reflect on Praise
- ☐ Reflect on Perspective
- ☐ Reflect on Service
- ☐ Reflect on Magnifying the Lord
- ☐ Reflect on Journaling
- ☐ Sabbath Reflection

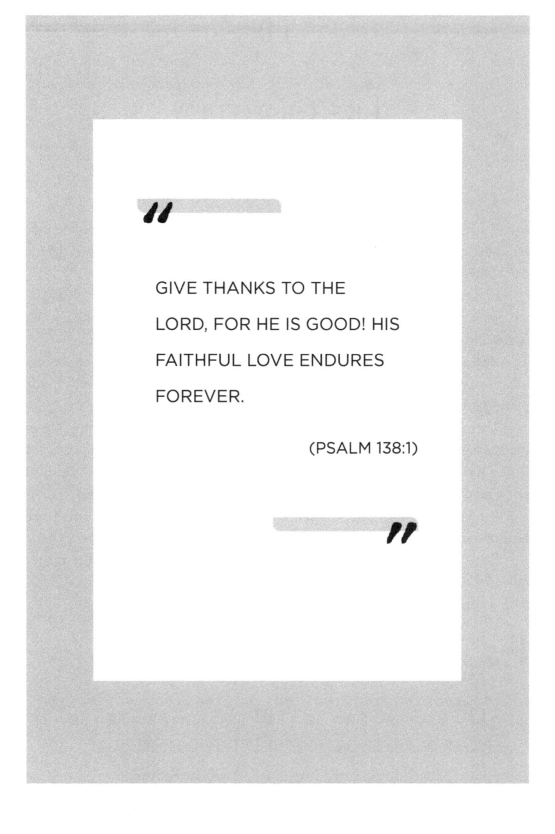

GIVE THANKS TO THE
LORD, FOR HE IS GOOD! HIS
FAITHFUL LOVE ENDURES
FOREVER.

(PSALM 138:1)

REFLECT ON PRAISE

It's been noted that the two most frequent prayers are "Please help!" and "Thank you!"—most of the time in that order!

Those are wonderful prayers, but what if we have them reversed? What if we practiced saying "Thank you" before "Please help"?

I read one time that "With prayers of gratitude, you can thank your way right into the presence of God."

Could it be that praise precedes plenty?

There is a verse that says that very thing:

> "May the peoples praise you, O God;
> may all the peoples praise you.
> Then the land will yield its harvest,
> and God, our God, will bless us."
> (Psalm 67:5-6 NIV)

What's interesting is that you don't have to feel like praising and thanking God to begin. Begin with the words, and the feelings follow.

READ THE VERSE ON THE OPPOSITE PAGE, THEN REPHRASE AND PERSONALIZE AS A PRAYER FROM YOU TO GOD.

Whether you *feel* grateful at the
moment, begin writing things you
know you are thankful for. Keep
writing until your emotions follow
your words. How long did it take?

When talking with friends, do you
spend more time talking about
your problems or your praises?

Think about a problem in your life
right now. Before it is solved, write
down praise to God for His love for
you, His awareness of all that you
are facing, and His faithfulness to
you every day.

MY "AHA"

Awaken

What passage or insight felt most personal for you?

Hear

What might God be saying to you?

Ask

Write a prayer asking God to help you praise him to bring blessing into your life or into the life of someone you know.

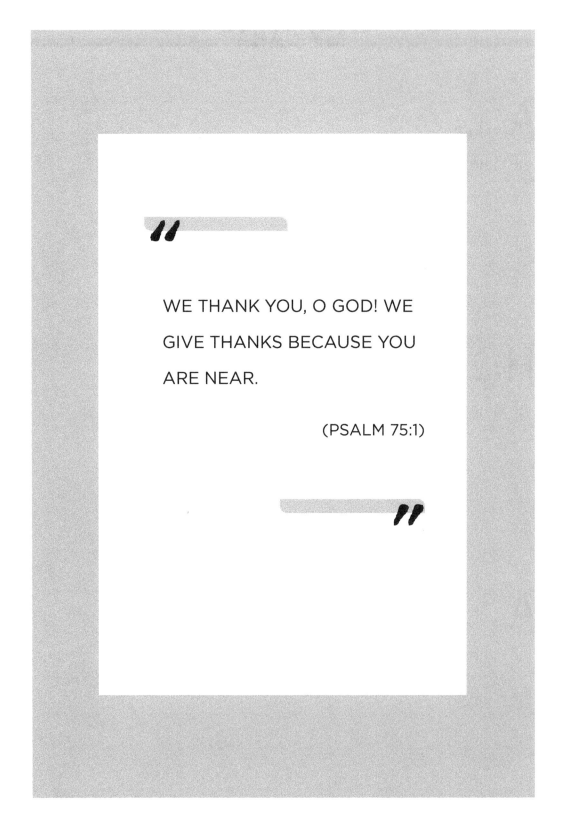

WE THANK YOU, O GOD! WE
GIVE THANKS BECAUSE YOU
ARE NEAR.

(PSALM 75:1)

Reflect on Perspective

If you are waiting for your life to get easier before telling God how grateful you are, you'll be waiting forever.

No one has a monopoly on hard. Most everyone is living their own version of hard right now. I'm in near daily conversations with leaders who feel overwhelming stress. One just told me that he's never had so much trouble sleeping. Another said he was exhausted by unrelenting challenges hitting his inbox and iPhone all day every day.

Everyone seems to be tired and longing for relief. I think I know why. The unrelenting uncertainty of our times is exhausting!

In ministry and in leadership roles of any sort, you're either coming out of a crisis, in the middle of a crisis or heading into a crisis. In some ways that's inevitable. The apostle Paul reminded us that "we must suffer many hardships to enter the kingdom of God" (Acts 14:22). Jesus told us, "Here on earth you will have many trials and sorrows" (John 16:33).

These days I encourage those I serve to remember that we are either coming out of a season of unspeakable blessing, in the middle of a season of unspeakable blessing, or heading into a season of unspeakable blessing. While hard knocks are inevitable, so is the blessing of the presence of God.

READ THE VERSE ON THE OPPOSITE PAGE, THEN REPHRASE AND PERSONALIZE AS A PRAYER FROM YOU TO GOD.

What are your thoughts on how
close you feel to God during
seasons of hardships versus
seasons of blessings?

Describe a time you spent time
praising and thanking God even
when life was less than perfect.
What did it do for you?

It's easy to feel like we're waiting
for the other shoe of crisis to drop.
What's looming around the corner?
Probably something bad, right? To
change your perspective, write a
prayer thanking God for the good
things he has waiting for you in
the near future!

MY "AHA"

Awaken

What passage or insight felt most personal for you?

Hear

What might God be saying to you?

Ask

Write a prayer asking God to help you focus on blessings over hardships to bring blessing into your life or into the life of someone you know.

"

GRATITUDE IS THE GAME
CHANGER THAT OPENS UP
BOTH OUR HEAD AND OUR
HEART TO GOD'S BLESSINGS
THAT SURROUND US AND
THOSE YET TO ARRIVE!

—ALAN AHLGRIM

"

Reflect on Service

Would you like to be more involved in helping, serving, and encouraging others? If so, you'll find the results of this study to be interesting.

Researchers randomly assigned people to three groups. Each group was asked to journal every day.

- Group one was asked to write about five major challenges.
- Group two was asked to write about five minor hassles.
- Group three was asked to write about five reasons for gratitude.

As we might predict, the gratitude group became the most grateful. But even more notable, the gratitude group was most likely to help others.

In short, journaling about gratefulness resulted in participants becoming more energetic, hopeful, and helpful. In other words, when people were more grateful, they had the greatest emotional capacity to help other people!

If you want to minister and serve others, increasing your gratitude for God's blessings in your own life is foundational!

Read the quote on the opposite page, then rephrase and personalize as a prayer from you to God.

Make a list of negative emotions
that seem to lose their power when
you fill yourself with gratitude.

Why do you think grateful people
are better equipped to serve
others?

Journaling is one way to increase
your attitude of gratitude. Can you
think of other ways?

MY "AHA"

Awaken

WHAT PASSAGE OR INSIGHT FELT MOST PERSONAL FOR YOU?

Hear

WHAT MIGHT GOD BE SAYING TO YOU?

Ask

WRITE A PRAYER ASKING GOD TO HELP YOU SERVE OTHERS TO BRING BLESSING INTO YOUR LIFE OR INTO THE LIFE OF SOMEONE YOU KNOW.

"

I CRY OUT TO GOD MOST
HIGH, TO GOD WHO WILL
FULFILL HIS PURPOSE FOR
ME. HE WILL SEND HELP
FROM HEAVEN TO RESCUE
ME.

(PSALM 57:2-3)

REFLECT ON MAGNIFYING THE LORD

Every day for the last few years, I've recorded five reasons I'm grateful to God. I'm finding that the more I focus my prayers on praise the more reasons I see to celebrate the goodness of God. In short, I'm magnifying Him and not my problems.

What do you want to magnify? While praying, journaling, and reflecting can seem to magnify our problems, praise only magnifies God.

"I will bless the Lord at all times; his praise shall continually be in my mouth … Oh, magnify the Lord with me, and let us exalt his name together" (Psalm 34:1,3 ESV).

What are the things you are grateful for today? A leader of another covenant group took this idea and started his own "Grateful 4" practice. Adam Turner writes four things every day that have brought him delight. King David wrote: "Let all that I am praise the Lord; may I never forget the good things he does for me" (Psalm 103:2).

R EAD THE VERSE ON THE OPPOSITE PAGE, THEN REPHRASE AND PERSONALIZE AS A PRAYER FROM YOU TO GOD.

What are your "Grateful 4" for today?

Even if it's not our intention, it's easy to magnify our problems. What are some of the ways you tend to do that?

Ponder David's words, "I will bless the Lord at all times; his praise shall continually be in my mouth." How could you make these words true in your own life?

MY "AHA"

Awaken

WHAT PASSAGE OR INSIGHT FELT MOST PERSONAL FOR YOU?

Hear

WHAT MIGHT GOD BE SAYING TO YOU?

Ask

WRITE A PRAYER ASKING GOD TO HELP YOU MAGNIFY HIS NAME TO BRING BLESSING INTO YOUR LIFE OR INTO THE LIFE OF SOMEONE YOU KNOW.

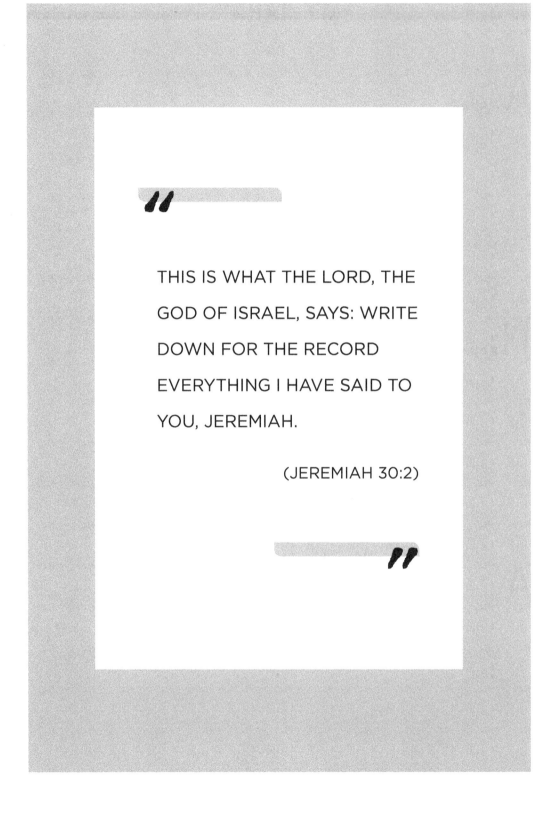

"

THIS IS WHAT THE LORD, THE
GOD OF ISRAEL, SAYS: WRITE
DOWN FOR THE RECORD
EVERYTHING I HAVE SAID TO
YOU, JEREMIAH.

(JEREMIAH 30:2)

"

REFLECT ON JOURNALING

Did you know that journaling can rewire your brain? That's one of the most powerful lessons I've learned in recent years. I once used my journal space to scribble about frustrations or difficulties. Now I find that focusing on gratitude improves my disposition, and writing my "gratitudes" improves my memory!

You're probably not as smart as you think you are. Studies are now documenting that computers are not making us smarter. In fact, it's just the opposite. It turns out that the act of physically putting pen to paper helps us to better remember. Yes, that means writing long-hand with a pen.

One psychologist concluded, "When we write, a unique neural circuit is automatically activated." I find that intriguing. In this day of technological addiction, we are losing our capacity for retention. Many don't even think that physically writing much of anything is important anymore. Think again.

While computers can retrieve information for us, computers cannot reflect. The psalmist said, "I pondered the direction of my life" (Psalm 119:59). How long has it been since you *pondered* something?

If you're ready to enjoy the benefits of reflecting and retaining, pick up a pen and write!

READ THE VERSE ON THE OPPOSITE PAGE, THEN REPHRASE AND PERSONALIZE AS A PRAYER FROM YOU TO GOD.

You've probably been writing in longhand in this journal. Are you ready for more? Spend ten minutes writing about the three of the most important lessons you have learned using this *Discovery Journal*. (If you need more space, there are blank journal pages in the back of this book.)

Are you more of an internal processor or a verbal processor? How does the act of writing work with either personality style? Do you prefer to reflect with the writing of complete sentences and paragraphs or simply with bullets? Which style best helps you to disentangle your thoughts, both for your benefit and for the benefit of others?

How might this journal become a long-term companion for you? If you were participating in another discussion group using the *Soul Strength* book, would you prefer to start a fresh journal or to review this one? Why?

MY "AHA"

Awaken

What passage or insight felt most personal for you?

Hear

What might God be saying to you?

Ask

Write a prayer asking God to help harness the power of journaling to bring blessing into your life or into the life of someone you know.

SABBATH REFLECTION

Soul work is slow work

WHAT IS *DELIGHTING* YOU?

WHAT IS *DRAINING* YOU?

WHAT ARE YOU *DISCOVERING*?

WHAT ARE YOU *DETERMINING* TO DO?

WERE ANY OF YOUR ANSWERS INFLUENCED BY YOUR RECENT READINGS? IF SO, HOW?

11

FINISH WITH BLESSING

Read Chapter 11 from the companion book Soul Strength: Rhythms for Thriving.

Early one morning I was reading and reflecting on the final moments of Christ's life on earth.

After the resurrection, the Lord shared the Great Commission with his disciples and friends and explained what was about to unfold with the sending of the Holy Spirit to be with them.

"Then Jesus led them to Bethany, and lifting his hands to heaven, he blessed them. While he was blessing them, he left them and was taken up to heaven" (Luke 24-50-51).

When I read that it hit me, "What a way to go!"

A buddy of mine just experienced this prior to the passing of a close friend. The final words of his devoted friend were these: "David, see you on the other side!" With his final words, Kim literally left a blessing behind. That's the way I want to go!

We ought to live every day with the awareness that it could be our last, because one day it certainly will be.

ENJOY THE FOLLOWING REFLECTIONS:

- ☐ Reflect on Transitions
- ☐ Reflect on Burnout
- ☐ Reflect on Loss
- ☐ Reflect on Opportunity
- ☐ Reflect on Peace of Mind
- ☐ Sabbath Reflection

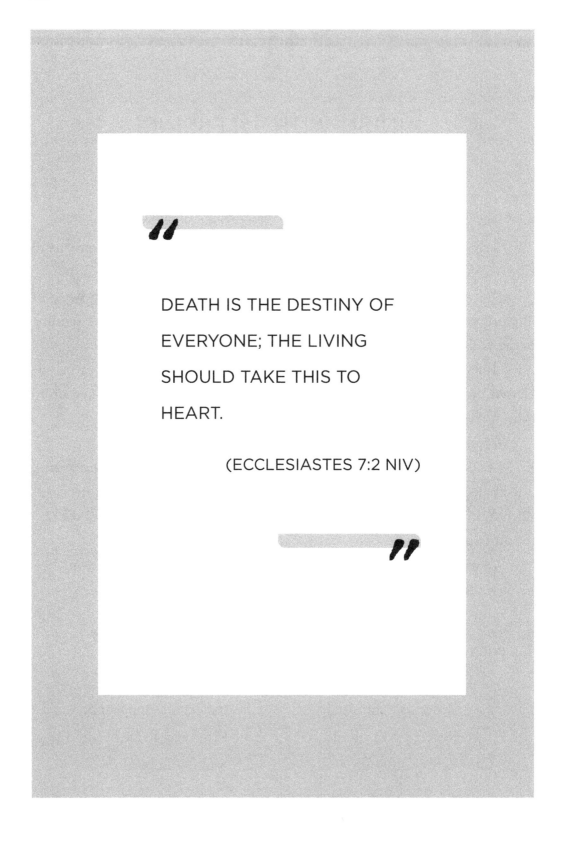

"

DEATH IS THE DESTINY OF
EVERYONE; THE LIVING
SHOULD TAKE THIS TO
HEART.

(ECCLESIASTES 7:2 NIV)

"

REFLECT ON TRANSITIONS

You may be a pastor, a leader in your company, a parent, or a police officer. Maybe you are a full-time student, retiree, caregiver, or athlete. But whatever your role or stage in life, there's one thing you can count on: a transition is in your future.

Psychologist Henry Cloud's insightful 2011 book entitled *Necessary Endings* provides excellent vocabulary that helps us embrace the inevitable:

> "Whether we like it or not, endings are part of life. They are woven into the fabric of life itself, both when it goes well and also when it doesn't. On the good side of life, for us to ever get to a new level, a new tomorrow, or the next step, something has to end. Life has seasons, stages, and phases. For there to be anything new, old things always have to end, and we have to let go of them. Endings are not only part of life; they are requirement for living and thriving, professionally and personally."

READ THE VERSE ON THE OPPOSITE PAGE, THEN REPHRASE AND PERSONALIZE AS A PRAYER FROM YOU TO GOD.

In this season in your life, what is currently drawing to a close? How do you feel about this?

What is beginning? How do you feel about this?

Share your thoughts on grieving an ending while looking forward to something new.

MY "AHA"

Awaken

WHAT PASSAGE OR INSIGHT FELT MOST PERSONAL FOR YOU?

Hear

WHAT MIGHT GOD BE SAYING TO YOU?

Ask

WRITE A PRAYER ASKING GOD TO HELP YOU NAVIGATE ENDINGS AND BEGINNINGS IN ORDER TO BRING BLESSING INTO YOUR LIFE OR INTO THE LIFE OF SOMEONE YOU KNOW.

IF YOU KNEW THAT
DEATH WOULD HAPPEN
TOMORROW, HOW WOULD
YOU LIVE TODAY? THAT
IS THE WHOLE POINT OF
ECCLESIASTES.

—DAVID GIBSON

REFLECT ON BURNOUT

Believe it or not, most people who enter ministry—even with great enthusiasm—eventually drop out. The dropout rate is about fifty percent within the first five years, and then it gets worse! Only about ten percent of those who remain after the initial glow wears off remain active in ministry for the full run. Just ten percent!

In short, most Christian leaders who start well don't finish that way. Why? At the risk of generalizing too much let me offer a few reasons:

- Inadequate support: they feel under paid and under affirmed by those they seek to serve.
- Inadequate disciplines: they fail to exercise spiritually and physically.
- Inadequate guardrails: they forget their humanity and naively succumb to the allure of forbidden fruit.
- Inadequate awareness: they forget they have an Enemy out to destroy them and all they hold dear.
- Inadequate friendships: they postpone building and servicing deep relationships with others to whom they can safely bare their soul.

READ THE QUOTE ON THE OPPOSITE PAGE, THEN REPHRASE AND PERSONALIZE AS A PRAYER FROM YOU TO GOD.

Does burnout always mean it's time to quit and move on to something new? What can you do to know if it's time to quit, take a break, or continue what you're doing with more support?

Whatever your profession or calling, if you were to create a plan to phase out and move into something new *before* burnout occurs, what would that look like?

Which of your accomplishments—current or future—do you think have the best chance of living on after you're gone?

MY "AHA"

WAKEN

WHAT PASSAGE OR INSIGHT FELT MOST PERSONAL FOR YOU?

H**EAR**

WHAT MIGHT GOD BE SAYING TO YOU?

A**SK**

WRITE A PRAYER ASKING GOD TO HELP YOU AVOID THE CHOICES THAT LEAD TO BURNOUT IN ORDER TO BRING BLESSING INTO YOUR LIFE OR INTO THE LIFE OF SOMEONE YOU KNOW.

"

THIS TIME I DON'T WANT TO
MAKE JUST A SHORT VISIT
AND THEN GO RIGHT ON. I
WANT TO COME AND STAY
AWHILE, IF THE LORD WILL
LET ME. . . . THERE IS A WIDE-
OPEN DOOR FOR A GREAT
WORK HERE, ALTHOUGH
MANY OPPOSE ME.

(I CORINTHIANS 16:7-9)

"

Reflect on Loss

Prior to my own transition out of pastoring a megachurch, I was warned that it would be harder and hurt more than expected. Grief is a complicated thing. However, by God's grace, the grief of any ending can open doors to new opportunities for all. What's essential is for leaders to embrace the transition rather than to resent it.

Grieving while leaving is common. Just as there is no perfect leader or organization, there can be no perfect leadership transition. Every church and organization is a unique combination of flawed people and challenging circumstances never to be repeated again.

I've learned that great gratitude is the greatest antidote to great grief. As I see it now, the more problems you have (or have had), the more potential you have to help others. God never wastes a pain that is given to Him. He lights our path one step at a time so that we can help light the path for others. As the psalmist said, "Light shines in the darkness for the godly" (Psalm 112:4).

Timing requires waiting and trusting. Endings can be both sad and scary, but in God's grand plan they can become beautiful new beginnings. As someone once said, "A sunset in one land is always a sunrise in another."

Read the verse on the opposite page, then rephrase and personalize as a prayer from you to God.

What endings in your life have you grieved? Do you have endings you are still grieving?

Share your thoughts on what grieving well should look like. Is that what you're experiencing?

Do you give yourself permission to grieve losses, or move quickly into busy-ness to avoid pain?

MY "AHA"

AWAKEN

WHAT PASSAGE OR INSIGHT FELT MOST PERSONAL FOR YOU?

HEAR

WHAT MIGHT GOD BE SAYING TO YOU?

ASK

WRITE A PRAYER ASKING GOD TO HELP YOU TRUST HIM AS YOU GRIEVE IN ORDER TO BRING BLESSING INTO YOUR LIFE OR INTO THE LIFE OF SOMEONE YOU KNOW.

NOW TO HIM WHO IS ABLE
TO DO IMMEASURABLY
MORE THAN ALL WE ASK OR
IMAGINE, ACCORDING TO HIS
POWER THAT IS AT WORK
WITHIN US.

(EPHESIANS 3:20-21 NIV)

REFLECT ON OPPORTUNITY

Timely transitions should not be feared as long as the transitioning leader is prepared and preparing those around him. As the season of transition approaches, many leaders hesitate and delay because they know they must have something to live on, and something to live for.

And yet, while transitions are seasons of great challenge, they are also seasons of wonderful opportunity. In fact, most of the miracles of the Bible are clustered around three transitions: Moses to Joshua, Elijah to Elisha, and Jesus to the apostles.

Relying on God to reveal the next opportunity in life—even if we don't see it yet—isn't easy. What if it's not what we imagined? What if it's not something we want to do? What if nothing appears?

How do we let go of what we have to grasp the next thing he has for us?

This is where our trust in Him comes into play.

READ THE VERSE ON THE OPPOSITE PAGE, THEN REPHRASE AND PERSONALIZE AS A PRAYER FROM YOU TO GOD.

What do you find easy to trust God
with? What is difficult?

What is on your bucket list? Do
you have unfulfilled dreams?
Could God be stirring up in your
spirit one of those nearly forgotten
dreams?

When you face transitions, who in
your community can you approach
for support and advice? Jot down
the names of friends and mentors
who can help you navigate the
current or next transition in your
life. Will you commit to reaching
out to them as the need arises?

MY "AHA"

WAKEN

WHAT PASSAGE OR INSIGHT FELT MOST PERSONAL FOR YOU?

HEAR

WHAT MIGHT GOD BE SAYING TO YOU?

ASK

WRITE A PRAYER ASKING GOD TO HELP YOU SEE HIS HAND IN EACH TRANSITION IN ORDER TO BRING BLESSING INTO YOUR LIFE OR INTO THE LIFE OF SOMEONE YOU KNOW.

FOR OUR PRESENT TROUBLES ARE SMALL AND WON'T LAST FOR LONG. YET THEY PRODUCE FOR US A GLORY THAT VASTLY OUTWEIGHS THEM AND WILL LAST FOREVER!

(2 CORINTHIANS 4:17)

REFLECT ON PEACE OF MIND

Comedian George Burns died at the age of ninety-nine. Shortly before his death he wrote:

> "There's an old saying, 'Life begins at 40.' That's silly. Life begins every morning when you wake up. Open your mind to it; don't just sit there, do things … the possibilities are endless. The point is, with a good positive attitude (and a little bit of luck) there's no reason why you can't live to be 100. And once you've done that you've really got it made because very few people die over 100!"

It's been said that the Christian life can be summarized in one word: *trust*.

Jesus said: "I am leaving you with a gift: peace of mind and heart. And the peace I give is a gift the world cannot give. So don't be troubled or afraid" (John 14:27).

The future is nothing to fear. God is already there waiting for you to arrive. As C. S. Lewis once said, "There are far, far better things ahead than any we leave behind."

READ THE VERSE ON THE OPPOSITE PAGE, THEN REPHRASE AND PERSONALIZE AS A PRAYER FROM YOU TO GOD.

What emotions do Jesus' words
"Don't be troubled or afraid"
evoke in you?

What things can you do that will
help you embrace and follow his
encouraging command?

You have probably heard other
believers share their own stories of
learning to trust God. Share one of
those stories now. Does that story
leave you encouraged?

MY "AHA"

Awaken

WHAT PASSAGE OR INSIGHT FELT MOST PERSONAL FOR YOU?

Hear

WHAT MIGHT GOD BE SAYING TO YOU?

Ask

WRITE A PRAYER ASKING GOD TO HELP YOU EMBRACE PEACE OF MIND TO BRING BLESSING INTO YOUR LIFE OR INTO THE LIFE OF SOME-ONE YOU KNOW.

SABBATH REFLECTION

Soul work is slow work

WHAT IS *DELIGHTING* YOU?

WHAT IS *DRAINING* YOU?

WHAT ARE YOU *DISCOVERING*?

WHAT ARE YOU *DETERMINING* TO DO?

WERE ANY OF YOUR ANSWERS INFLUENCED BY YOUR RECENT READINGS? IF SO, HOW?

12

STOP PROCRASTINATING!

Read Chapter 12 from the companion book, Soul Strength: Rhythms for Thriving.

It's one thing to postpone a project like cleaning the closet or mowing the lawn and it's another to postpone the major investments of life:

- Building a career
- Saving for retirement
- Developing deep connections

We may say we desire these things and plan to do them one day, but good intentions are not enough. As King Solomon observed, "Good planning and hard work lead to prosperity" (Proverbs 21:5).

Our son just introduced me to his new neighbor, an immigrant from Uzbekistan. Not long after arriving to America a decade ago, he and his brother started their own security business which is now thriving in multiple locations.

When I asked him his secret he said, "It's really simple. Get up and go to work."

What might you need to work on today to enjoy a better life tomorrow?

ENJOY THE FOLLOWING REFLECTIONS:

- ☐ Reflect on Distractions
- ☐ Reflect on Love
- ☐ Reflect on Clarity
- ☐ Reflect on Priority and Productivity
- ☐ Reflect on Choosing Now
- ☐ Sabbath Reflection

"

DESPITE THEIR DESIRES, THE
LAZY WILL COME TO RUIN,
FOR THEIR HANDS REFUSE
TO WORK.

(PROVERBS 21:25)

"

Reflect on Distractions

A friend of ours says that her ninth-grade son earned an A+ in procrastination!

Most of us know exactly what that is. We fully intend to schedule that conversation or read that book or start that project, just not right now. Then before we know it, *not right now* becomes *not ever*.

On the other hand, there are men like Nehemiah who determine to ignore the distractions and pursue the project no matter what.

If you'll recall the biblical account, Nehemiah was seized with the need to rebuild the walls of Jerusalem—so much so that he sought the permission of a pagan king to take on the effort. This passionate and purpose-filled man had many adversaries seeking to distract him. Then, at one critical moment recorded in Nehemiah 6, he said, "I am carrying on a great project, and I cannot go down. Why should the work stop while I leave it and go down to you?"

We all live with unrelenting distractions that can combine together to keep us from pursuing God's best.

There will never be a day without distractions, nor a day without the opportunity to repeatedly begin again! A work in progress is still progress. Something is better than nothing. We can't do it all, but we can do something by starting now!

R EAD THE VERSE ON THE OPPOSITE PAGE, THEN REPHRASE AND PERSONALIZE AS A PRAYER FROM YOU TO GOD.

Efficiency is doing things right;
effectiveness is doing the right
things. Which is the greater
challenge for you?

What unfinished project is staring
you in the face right now? What is
keeping you from addressing and
completing it?

What drives you more: Crisis or
opportunity? Calendar or cause?
The fear of failure, or the reward
of a project well done?

MY "AHA"

A<small>WAKEN</small>

W<small>HAT PASSAGE OR INSIGHT FELT MOST PERSONAL FOR YOU?</small>

H<small>EAR</small>

W<small>HAT MIGHT</small> G<small>OD BE SAYING TO YOU?</small>

A<small>SK</small>

W<small>RITE A PRAYER ASKING</small> G<small>OD TO HELP YOU STAY THE COURSE IN ORDER TO BRING BLESSING INTO YOUR LIFE OR INTO THE LIFE OF SOMEONE YOU KNOW.</small>

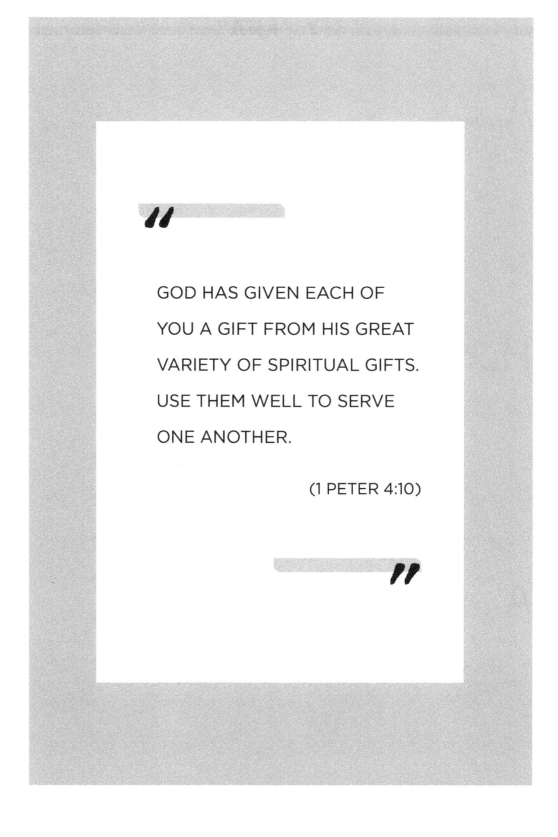

"

GOD HAS GIVEN EACH OF
YOU A GIFT FROM HIS GREAT
VARIETY OF SPIRITUAL GIFTS.
USE THEM WELL TO SERVE
ONE ANOTHER.

(1 PETER 4:10)

"

REFLECT ON LOVE

I was feeling convicted recently about procrastinating while finishing this book when I came across this question by Tim Keller:

"Is there a project you have not been able to finish? Stir up your love for the people who would benefit from it, look to the 'Finisher of our faith' (Hebrews 12:2) and finish it."

His words resonated with me.

What a difference in perspective!

When we are motivated by love, we tackle obstacles with confidence. We don't give up. We are driven by new levels of energy and focus. We experience greater joy and satisfaction when the task is complete.

When we find ourselves putting off a task or responsibility, a shift in perspective can be the key to seeing it through to completion. Look past the task to the people who will benefit. Let your love for them provide the wind in your sails.

READ THE VERSE ON THE OPPOSITE PAGE, THEN REPHRASE AND PERSONALIZE AS A PRAYER FROM YOU TO GOD.

Are you motivated more by duty
or love? How has that been
illustrated in your life recently?

What is love prompting you to do
this week with a work challenge,
a family challenge, a relationship
challenge?

Andy Stanley asks the question:
"What does love require of me?"
Dare to ask God that question
right now and then ask God to
help you discern what He might
be prompting you to do about it.
Write that down. What feelings
come to mind?

MY "AHA"

Awaken

WHAT PASSAGE OR INSIGHT FELT MOST PERSONAL FOR YOU?

Hear

WHAT MIGHT GOD BE SAYING TO YOU?

Ask

WRITE A PRAYER ASKING GOD TO HELP YOU BE MOTIVATED BY LOVE IN ORDER TO BRING BLESSING INTO YOUR LIFE OR INTO THE LIFE OF SOMEONE YOU KNOW.

"

WE ARE NOT UNCERTAIN
OF GOD, JUST UNCERTAIN
OF WHAT HE IS GOING TO
DO NEXT.... WHEN WE HAVE
THE RIGHT RELATIONSHIP
WITH GOD, LIFE IS FULL OF
SPONTANEOUS, JOYFUL
UNCERTAINTY AND
EXPECTANCY.

—OSWALD CHAMBERS

"

REFLECT ON CLARITY

I just reread the highlights of one of my favorite books, *Ruthless Trust*. Author Brennan Manning tells how John Kavanaugh went to work with Mother Teresa for three months at the House of the Dying in Calcutta.

On their first morning working together she asked, "And what can I do for you?" Kavanaugh simply asked her to pray for him.

"What do you want me to pray for?" she asked.

He humbly replied, "Pray that I have clarity."

She said firmly, "No, I will not do that."

When he asked her why, she said, "Clarity is the last thing you are clinging to and must let go of."

When Kavanaugh commented that she always seemed to have the clarity he longed for, she laughed and said, "I have never had clarity; what I have always had is trust. So I will pray that you trust God."

READ THE QUOTE ON THE OPPOSITE PAGE, THEN REPHRASE AND PERSONALIZE AS A PRAYER FROM YOU TO GOD.

While clarity is a good thing, the
need for clarity can get in in the
way of moving forward. What
are your thoughts on the tension
between clarity and trust?

It's been said that we should work
as if everything depends upon us
and pray as if everything depends
upon God. Which are you more
inclined to do, work or pray? How
could the next week be different if
you prayed daily over your to-do list?

What is the source of your
motivation and reward? The task
itself? The applause of others?
God? All of the above? Consider
each source. Does it feel life-
giving or draining?

MY "AHA"

Awaken

What passage or insight felt most personal for you?

Hear

What might God be saying to you?

Ask

Write a prayer asking God to help you value trust over clarity to bring blessing into your life or into the life of someone you know.

JESUS SAID:

BUT SEEK FIRST HIS
KINGDOM AND HIS
RIGHTEOUSNESS, AND ALL
THESE THINGS WILL BE
GIVEN TO YOU AS WELL.

(MATTHEW 6:33 NIV)

REFLECT ON PRIORITY AND PRODUCTIVITY

Years ago, Charles Schwab confronted a management consultant with an unusual challenge. "Show me a way to get more things done, and if it works, I'll pay anything within reason."

The consultant then handed him a piece of paper and had him write down the things he needed to do the next day. After that he had him number them in order of priority.

Then he said, "Tomorrow begin with item one and don't move on until you've finished it. Then everyday do the same thing. Make a list, put things in order of priority and begin at the top. After you've done that for several weeks, just send me a check for whatever you think it's worth."

A few weeks later the consultant received a surprisingly large check with a note from Charles Schwab saying that this little exercise was the most profitable lesson he had ever learned in his entire business career!

R EAD THE VERSE ON THE OPPOSITE PAGE, THEN REPHRASE AND PERSONALIZE AS A PRAYER FROM YOU TO GOD.

Is your workspace orderly or in chaos? How does the environment in which you work impact your productivity?

If you could design the workspace of your dreams, what would it look like? Are there improvements you can make from the color and décor of the room to the comfort of the furniture?

What methods have you used successfully that help you remain focused and undistracted on the assignments and projects given to you?

MY "AHA"

Awaken

What passage or insight felt most personal for you?

Hear

What might God be saying to you?

Ask

Write a prayer asking God to help you pursue his priorities in order to bring blessing into your life or into the life of someone you know.

"

THEY ALL CRIED AS THEY
EMBRACED AND KISSED
HIM GOOD-BYE. THEY WERE
SAD MOST OF ALL BECAUSE
HE HAD SAID THAT THEY
WOULD NEVER SEE HIM
AGAIN.

(ACTS 20:36-38)

"

Reflect on Choosing Now

I can't encourage you enough to stop procrastinating and start choosing the better thing, right now.

And one of the best things you can choose to do is intentionally create environments and embrace relationships that will strengthen your soul.

We don't need another book, conference, or academic degree. We need to know in the center of our soul that we are known, loved, and accepted.

That's the key to thriving!

For myself—and hundreds of leaders I've worked with—a key to thriving has been found in covenant groups. These soul-enriching small groups create the opportunity for connection, authenticity, growth, and transformation.

Unfortunately, getting started with a small group is one of those things that is easy to put off. It rarely feels like an urgency for anyone. That's why many people postpone it indefinitely! It's not because they don't intend to do it *someday*, it's just that the ideal day rarely arrives.

Whether you visit covenantconnections.life and begin or join a covenant group, or pursue a small group under a different model, connections that go deep will be the secret sauce to any transformation you long to make in your life.

READ THE VERSE ON THE OPPOSITE PAGE, THEN REPHRASE AND PERSONALIZE AS A PRAYER FROM YOU TO GOD.

Do you have three close friends
you could call at any time? Name
them and recall the last time you
had a meaningful conversation
with each of them.

Who would weep if they knew they
were talking to you for the last
time?

In light of life's uncertainties,
do you ever consider that every
conversational opportunity could
be your last? How might doing
so help you to better treasure the
time you have?

MY "AHA"

AWAKEN

WHAT PASSAGE OR INSIGHT FELT MOST PERSONAL FOR YOU?

HEAR

WHAT MIGHT GOD BE SAYING TO YOU?

ASK

WRITE A PRAYER ASKING GOD TO HELP YOU CHOOSE TO TAKE ACTION NOW IN A WAY THAT WILL BRING BLESSING INTO YOUR LIFE OR INTO THE LIFE OF SOMEONE YOU KNOW.

SABBATH REFLECTION

Soul work is slow work

WHAT IS *DELIGHTING* YOU?

WHAT IS *DRAINING* YOU?

WHAT ARE YOU *DISCOVERING*?

WHAT ARE YOU *DETERMINING* TO DO?

WERE ANY OF YOUR ANSWERS INFLUENCED BY YOUR RECENT
READINGS? IF SO, HOW?

ABOUT THE AUTHOR

Alan Ahlgrim has spent over half his life in Colorado. He is the father of three married children and six grandchildren. He and his wife for life, Linda, thoroughly enjoy an active life, hiking, kayaking, biking, and walking together with their Australian Labradoodle, Molly Brown, the Dog of Renown!

Alan served twenty-nine years as the founding pastor of Rocky Mountain Christian Church in Colorado, as well as helped to energize a national resurgence of church planting. He is now leveraging the agony and ecstasy of fifty years of ministry in his encore role as Founder and Chief Soul Care Officer of Covenant Connections.

Alan invests heavily in the hard work of heart work, helping other leaders serve well and finish well by connecting them in soul-enriching covenant groups. These small, in-depth communities are transformational and produce remarkable renewal and resilience. For more information visit covenantconnections.life.